Solo Jazz Piano
The Linear Approach

2nd Edition

Neil Olmstead

Edited by Jonathan Feist

Berklee Media

Associate Vice President: Dave Kusek
Director of Content: Debbie Cavalier
Business Manager: Linda Chady Chase
Technology Manager: Mike Serio
Marketing Manager—Berkleemusic: Barry Kelly
Senior Designer: David Ehlers

Berklee Press

Senior Writer/Editor: Jonathan Feist
Writer/Editor: Susan Gedutis
Production Manager: Shawn Girsberger
Marketing Manager—Berklee Press: Jennifer Rassler
Product Marketing Manager: David Goldberg
Production Assistants: Dan Chen and Louis O'Choa

ISBN 978-0-87639-120-4

DISTRIBUTED BY

HAL•LEONARD®
CORPORATION
7777 W. BLUEMOUND RD. P.O. BOX 13819
MILWAUKEE, WISCONSIN 53213

1140 Boylston Street
Boston, MA 02215-3693 USA
(617) 747-2146

Visit Berklee Press Online at
www.berkleepress.com

Visit Hal Leonard Online at
www.halleonard.com

With deepest admiration, love, and appreciation for her unending support of my career in music, this book is dedicated to Valerie Montgomery, my mother.

Contents

CD Tracks

Foreword

For the improvising pianist, a deep understanding of root, bass, and inversional harmonic relationships is absolutely essential. We benefit by understanding harmonic relationships and the strong implications and tonal gravity of the root structure and its generated harmonic overtones. With considerable alacrity, Neil Olmstead's fine work demonstrates and details a comprehensive palette and view of tonal harmony. He expounds upon this harmonic foundation with bass-line movements of nearly every possible style and level of difficulty, as well as melodic intricacy.

This volume offers the beginning improviser a step-by-step approach to improvising in a solo jazz context. It is equally valuable to the more advanced thinker who already has achieved some knowledge of chord changes, progressions of many kinds, and standard repertory. Much of Olmstead's fascinating presentation is immediately within reach of any pianist with a basic technique. Some materials will require more practice–particularly in regards to piano technique and the understanding of the tonal possibilities (e.g., pedal point and reharmonization) inherent in the piano's seemingly endless sonic potential. But any pianist will benefit by the journey that Olmstead has set forth.

An extremely important overall feature of Olmstead's work is the assertion of how one's melodic-linear language is enriched and extended by way of understanding bass-line movement on the keyboard. These concepts can be translated to other genres, such as contrabass, or used as a compositional tool for orchestration and tonal development on an even larger scale. Solo piano improvisation is the model, but it is also just the beginning.

With this understanding, and the clear manner in which Olmstead lays out his materials and avoids lengthy verbal descriptions, neologisms, and the like, the sky *is* the limit. The serious student of these materials cannot help but to be inspired and stimulated towards a deeper and deeper understanding. The tonal-harmonic universe, the mysteries of melodic development, and the essential concepts of composition are all filtered through the development of the bass-line phenomena. It is wonderfully presented in this extensive treatise on solo jazz improvisation.

William Thomas McKinley

William Thomas McKinley is a composer, pianist and educator who has performed with and/or written for Gary Burton, Eddie Gomez, Miroslav Vitous, Stan Getz, Joe Lovano, John Scofield, Roy Haynes, and many others. He lives on the North Shore of Massachusetts with his wife Marlene.

Acknowledgments

Thanks to the following people for their valued contributions to this effort.

Debbie Cavalier, Vice President of Online Learning and Continuing Education at Berklee Media, for her kind and inspired encouragement.

Jonathan Feist, Editor in Chief of Berklee Press, for his consistently detailed analysis and organization of content.

The staff at Berklee Press for their work in preparing the manuscript.

Sandy Letendre for her photographic expertise.

Peter Kontrimas for his artistic approach and technical expertise in recording the CD.

Jean McKenna O'Donnell and Scott McKenzie for their resources on Dave McKenna.

William Thomas McKinley for his thoughtful review and foreword.

My students of *Contrapuntal Jazz Improvisation for Pianists* for their detailed transcriptions and performances of this music.

Lennie Tristano for his unrelenting musical conviction and integrity, especially on his performance of "C Minor Complex," the improvisation that inspired this journey.

Dave McKenna for his joyful deep swing on hundreds of tunes that so encouraged me and my students to realize, "It can be done!"

And my wife, Donna Olmstead, for all her support and patience throughout this endeavor.

Introduction

Contrapuntal Jazz Improvisation

Contrapuntal jazz improvisation means improvising simultaneous lines of music within a jazz context. Typically, it is comprised of a bass line in the left hand and either a melody or improvised line in the right hand. This can be done within a jazz tune over chord changes or as a pure free-flowing improvisation devoid of specific form. In either case, it is a linear texture with wonderful possibilities in all manner of rhythm, harmony, and counterpoint.

History

Lennie Tristano was the groundbreaking pianist of this style with his *Descent Into the Maelstrom* (1952) and *The New Tristano* (1962) LPs. The latter recording contains superb performances of Lennie playing jazz standards as well as free-form improvisations. Subsequent recordings include *Concert in Copenhagen* of 1965 and numerous reissued tracks on various CDs. Lennie's musical character is rhythmically unique and intellectually complex, and it proved to be a driving force in the development of jazz.

The Boston pianist Dave McKenna could be considered the rhythmic antithesis of Lennie Tristano. His solo piano texture is also essentially contrapuntal, but with a more traditional swing. Many of Dave's solo and duo recordings contain wonderful examples of walking bass lines with deep-swinging, hard-driving right-hand improvisations rooted in the bebop tradition. McKenna's solo and duo piano discography is extensive and rooted in this tradition of playing.

Other pianists that have recorded in this contrapuntal style include Alan Broadbent, Connie Crothers (both students of Tristano's), Tete Monteliu, Kenny Baron, and Diana Krall. More rarely, we also find recordings of Oscar Peterson and Bill Evans playing great bass lines in solo and duo settings.

More evident today is the use of contrapuntal improvisation in ensemble settings. Pianists Brad Melhdau, Ken Werner, and Keith Jarrett are playing clear independent lower lines in the left hand that are set against traditional upper-voice improvised lines.

Appendix B. "Discography" lists some classic recordings in this style, and I encourage you to listen to them while studying these techniques.

The Text

This approach to teaching contrapuntal jazz piano has been refined over many years, teaching hundreds of pianists at Berklee College of Music. *Solo Jazz Piano* codifies this method. Each chapter includes a series of steps that will help develop the language needed to improvise contrapuntally. Left-hand vocabulary, right-hand chords, independence exercises, and ideas on arranging and improvisation are all described in detail. Part I reviews chord interpretation. Part II begins the contrapuntal journey. Starting with half-note bass lines, you will develop your sense of rhythmic independence and flexibility, and then move onto more sophisticated walking bass lines. Part III topics include left-hand motivic embellishment, pedal point, multi-voice improvisation, metric modulation, and motivic development.

Though the text touches on harmony, comping, solo development, and other techniques of improvisation, the focus is on contrapuntal techniques for the solo pianist.

How to Use This Book

Each chapter begins with a discussion of some theory or technique for improvising. These are supported by practice exercises, such as the *arrow sheets,* which will guide you through the thought process of using the technique. The exercises are followed by tunes, which are based on chord progressions of jazz standards. These tunes are presented in two different ways. *Etudes* are through-composed studies, based on various jazz standards. Every note is notated, and they serve as complete models for how the concepts presented earlier can be used. *Lead sheets* present only the melody and chord changes, and are more representative of what jazz players actually read from. You should create your own bass line, comping part, improvisation, and arrangement to these tunes, again, using the techniques and ideas discussed in the chapter. The accompanying CD provides examples of how some of the lead sheets might be interpreted. I encourage you to research the original tunes as well.

The Motives

Bass-line *motives* (short melodic ideas) are the prime source of vocabulary for the left hand. They originate from frequently used melodic shapes of the jazz tradition. They are not intellectually challenging; they are *functional,* allowing the bass line to move logically from chord to chord without distracting the performer from his creative right-hand improvisations. These motives should be memorized in much the same manner as you would memorize chord voicings, thereby always having something "in your fingers" to play throughout the harmonic progression of the tune.

When you study these lines, you may wonder, for example, why is this particular motive recommended:

. . . when this one could be used?

They are both valid musical ways of getting from the C-7 to the F7 chord. However, the more subtle, less patternistic shape of the first motive is preferred because the line can then be functional without sounding sequential, if the motive is repeated.

Specific methods of developing these motives and creating more diverse and interesting left-hand lines are introduced gradually.

How Piano Bass Lines Differ from String Bass Lines

Piano bass lines differ from string bass lines in that the clarity of the piano tone does not lend itself immediately to all the subtleties of the traditional bass instruments. Consequently, the bass motives discussed in this method are slightly different than those of a bass method. Where a bassist can get away with playing a large number of arpeggios, for example, the arpeggiated bass line on the piano can easily sound overdone and uninteresting, and possibly more "Chopinesque" than jazz oriented.

The Range

Additionally, the range of the bass line is important. The string bass sounds an octave lower than written and has an appropriate tone in almost all octaves. However, the piano bass line can easily sound too high. Hence, I encourage you to play bass lines that are lower than what you may initially feel is natural. This depth of sound is important for the right-hand line as well; the tenor range on the piano will fill in the overtones and significantly enhance the texture when only two voices are sounding. Both Lennie Tristano and Dave McKenna play many of their solos in this low, tenor range, sometimes never reaching the C above middle C.

Necessary Basics

Students of these concepts will gain greater confidence and ease in contrapuntal improvisation if they have:

- the ability to read grand-staff piano scores (see the etudes);

- a basic understanding of jazz chord structure and nomenclature (see chapter 1);

- a general aural concept of bebop piano style (see appendix B);

- a beginning knowledge of the repertoire;

- a functional knowledge of jazz terminology, scales, and modes;

- and most importantly, a strong desire to enhance and explore the contrapuntal possibilities of solo jazz piano technique.

Enjoy this book. I hope that it inspires you to be more creative in your own soloing.

PART I. Chords

Chord theory and its musical application lie at the heart of jazz. Chords provide the harmonic backdrop to all jazz standards and the harmonic framework for improvisation. It is therefore of paramount importance for students of jazz to learn chord structure and vocabulary thoroughly.

The Pianist's Role

In jazz, the pianist's role is to provide the tune's harmonic basis by playing the "changes" (chords) behind a soloist or his own solos. Pianists must have a variety of "voicings" (chord note arrangements) at their disposal.

Part I explores many common chord voicings and progressions found in jazz tunes. It also discusses aspects of "voice leading" through the changes, which enables your chords to have a linear quality.

Practice all these early exercises thoroughly. They will build your fluency in the harmonic language of jazz, and help you become a well-versed accompanist and an inspired soloist.

Chapter 1. Fundamentals of Chord Theory
Lead Sheet Basics

THEORY

Jazz pianists generally read from lead sheets. A lead sheet just has the melody and chord symbols. It is the pianist's job to interpret the lead sheet, creating a bass part, chords, melody, arrangement, rhythmic feel, and so on.

Follow this approach whenever you practice a lead sheet.

1. **Play just the melody.** Below is an example of lead sheet notation. When you use a lead sheet to create your own arrangement, begin by playing the melody alone.

2. **Play the melody and a simple bass part.** Once you can play the melody easily, add a simple bass line. The simplest bass line to play is the chord root, played once, held until the next chord symbol.

3. **Play the melody, bass, and inner chord notes.** Harmonize the melody by adding chord tones. This gives the melody a fuller sound and expresses more of the chord quality.

4. **Play the melody over chords.** While the right hand plays the melody, the left hand plays chords.

This approach will give you a complete sense of the melody and harmony, and it will help prepare you to create your own arrangement and improvisation of the tune. We will study techniques for developing lead sheets throughout this book.

Interpreting Chord Symbols

To learn a tune from a lead sheet, you must know the chords. Most jazz harmonies are based on seventh chords. Though seventh-chord symbols are not standardized, they all have three basic kinds of information. First, a letter indicates the chord root. Second, if the basic triad is not major, then a symbol follows that indicates the chord quality and the type of seventh used. Third, numerals (4, 6, 9, 11, and 13) in the chord symbol indicate notes at intervals away from the root.

The following chart shows some common notation and composition for seventh chords.

Quality	Abbreviation	Symbol	Example	Structure
Major	Maj	Ma, Maj	CMaj7	Maj triad/Maj 7
Minor	min	−, mi, min	C−7	min triad/min 7
Minor 7 flat-5	min7(♭5)	−7(♭5), min7(♭5)	C−7(♭5)	dim triad/min 7
Dominant	dom	7	C7	Maj triad/min 7
Augmented	aug	+	C+7	aug triad/min 7
Diminished	dim	°	C°7	dim triad/dim 7

Play the following *chord voicings* (arrangement of chord notes), observing the chord symbols.

Additional Notes on Chords

On dominant chord symbols, there may be a "4," indicating a suspended fourth. With these chords, the chord's third is replaced with the fourth, as in C7sus4.

Some chords include the numbers 9, 11, and/or 13, which indicate additional tones to the seventh chord. The numbers represent intervals from the chord root. These notes are called *tensions* (short for "extensions"), and are often written in parentheses following the 7, as in CMaj7(9). On dominant chords, they may be preceded by a sharp or flat, indicating that they are *altered* notes, such as C7(♭9).

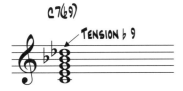

Play the following chord voicings, observing the tensions used. Note that the 9 replaces the root in the right-hand chords. The 13 replaces the 5 on the dominant chords. This technique is discussed in more detail in chapter 2.

This phrase includes three dominant seventh chords in common ways that they may be interpreted.

"Slash" Chord Symbols and Inversions

Two chord symbols separated by a slash (/) indicate a *composite* chord or an *inverted* chord. The letter after the slash indicates the bass note. For example, the GMaj7/B symbol is interpreted as a GMaj7 chord over the note B in the bass.

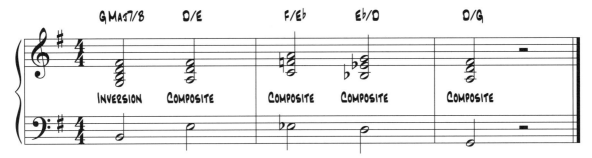

Comping

When accompanying another player, it is common to play chords in the right hand with a bass line in the left hand. This is called *comping* (short for "accompanying").

On piano, the range for these comping chord voicings is usually between the D below middle C and the B-flat above middle C.

When you create a comping part, you can use any of the notes in the chord. Always include the root, 3, and 7, but if the root is in your left hand's bass line, you may leave it—and sometimes the 5—out of your right-hand voicing. In your right hand, replace these omitted notes with tensions (9 for 1, 13 for 5).

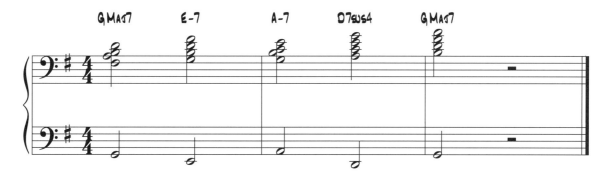

A *chord chart* is like a lead sheet, except that it indicates only the chords, without the melody. The slashes (/ / / /) mean "create your own part." Play the chords, improvising the inversions and rhythms.

Voice Leading

When moving from one chord to the next, try to minimize the motion. Look for common notes between the two chords, and when a voice must change, move to the closest note of the next chord. This motion of the voices is called *common-tone voice leading*. Generally, you will try to make the chord transitions as smooth as possible.

If the top notes of your voicings move by step, your voice leading will most likely be smooth. Always consider this melodic quality in your comping.

Below, compare the melodic character of the voice-led version to the second version.

Tip

One way to check your melodic content (and hence, voice leading) is by singing the top voice of your chords. Which of the above examples is more singable?

PRACTICE

Comping Practice

Practice these two chord charts in three different ways.

1. Play these chords in root position with your left hand.

2. Play them again with your right hand, and play the root note with your left hand. Substitute 9s freely in your right-hand voicings.

3. Play the progression, and try to make your voice leading as smooth as possible.

Exercise 1. Comping Practice

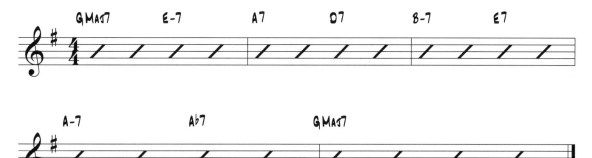

Exercise 2. Comping Practice

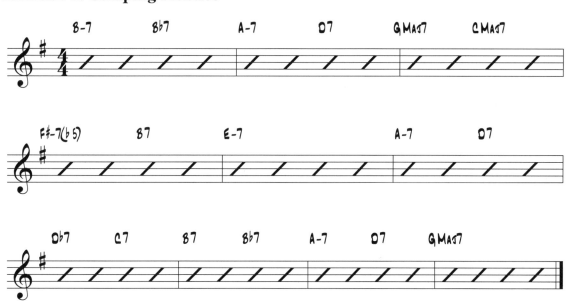

CHALLENGE

Repeat step (3) above. Can you replace the root in the right hand with a tension?

TUNES

Etude. "So Easily"

"So Easily" is based on the chord changes to "I Fall in Love Too Easily" by Jerome Kern. This piece illustrates a melody in the right hand with a variety of chords in the left hand (as you did in theory step 4 earlier this chapter). Note the different inversions used and the independent lines of harmony.

So Easily

Neil Olmstead

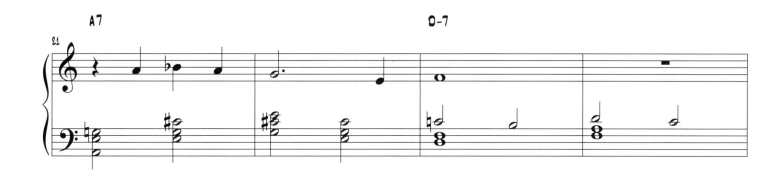

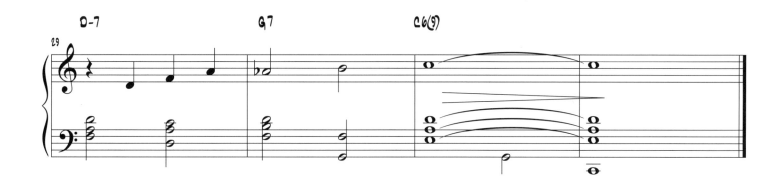

Lead Sheet. "So Easily"

This lead sheet is for the same tune as the etude. Create your own comping part using the chord symbols. Focus on rhythmic feel and voice leading. Use the CD for reference, as an example of how your arrangement might sound.

1. Play only the melody.

2. Play the melody with bass notes.

3. Play the melody, bass notes, and some inner harmony.

4. Play the melody in the right hand and chords in the left hand.

Chapter 2. Chord Extensions
Beyond the Basic Chord Tones

THEORY

In the fifties, pianists such as Red Garland and Bill Evans put more color into their harmonic language. Doubling the root and 5 sounded heavy and redundant, as the bass was playing those notes, so they began to replace the root and 5 with extensions to the chord, such as the 9 and 13, even when those extensions were not indicated on the lead sheet. We now generally refer to these notes as *tensions* (short for "extensions") and the process of using them as *tension substitution.*

Here are some common chords in their written form and then again, with tensions. In major and minor chords, the 9 is often substituted for the root, most often in first and third inversions.

In dominant chords, the 9 is often substituted for the root, and the 13 for the 5, commonly set in first and third inversions.

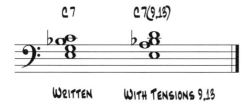

Altered Dominant

Because the dominant chord has the most dissonant function, the tensions are often *altered* (raised or lowered a half step), particularly in minor keys. Again, these are commonly set in first and third inversions.

Here are some common altered dominant-7 combinations:

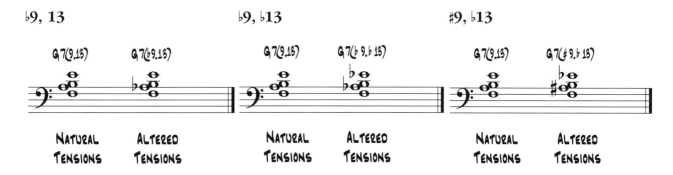

Practice these common left-hand voicings in all keys.

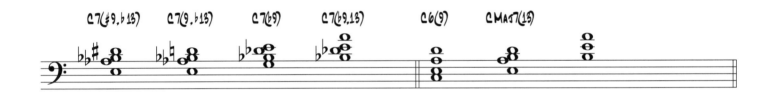

> **Tip**
>
> On major seventh and minor seventh chords, use tension 9 for 1 (root). On dominant seventh chords, use 9 for 1 and 13 for 5. These chords are often in first and third inversion.

PRACTICE

Chord Voicings

Exercise. Analysis of Extended Chords

Practice these chord voicings, adding the chord root in your left hand, as illustrated. They are all common voicings that can be used in your comping. Analyze each chord, circling and labeling the tensions, and indicating inversions. For example, the first one uses a tension 9, and it is in third inversion. Note that second inversion major 7 and minor 7 chords often have no tension.

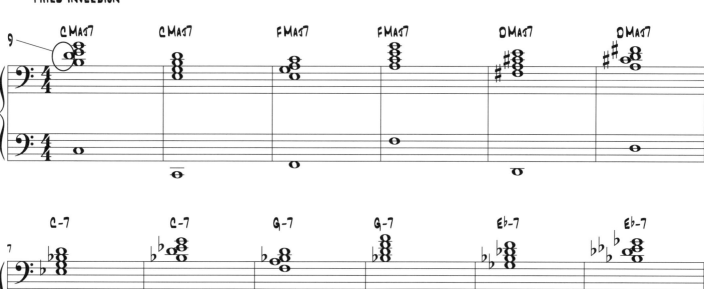

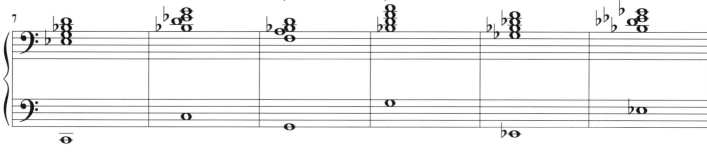

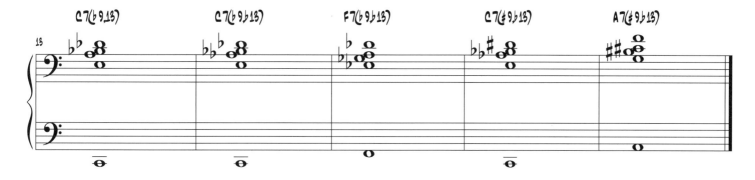

II V I Exercises

Going from the II to the V to the I chord (the chords built on the second, fifth, and tonic scale degrees) is among the most common progressions in jazz. These exercises will help develop your facility playing II V I progressions. Following the cue notes (top voice), continue the voice-leading pattern to the end.

Exercise 1. II V I in Major

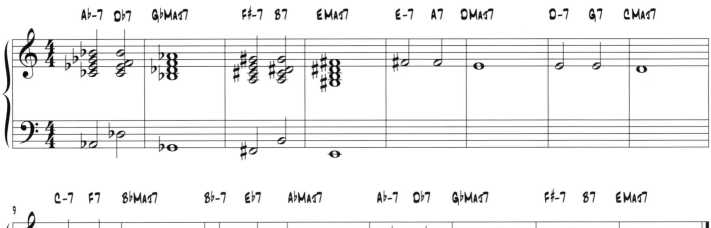

Exercise 2. II V I in Major

Exercise 3. II V I Major Chromatic Descent

Exercise 4. Left Hand Practice

Practice this next progression in your left hand only. After the first II V I, fill in the rest of the notes, using smooth voice leading.

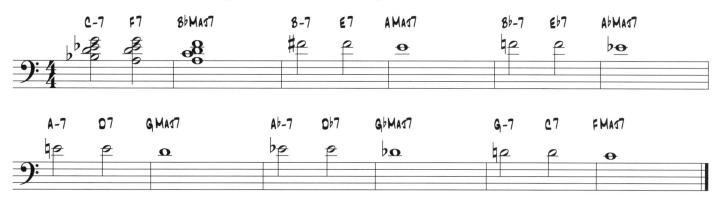

Exercise 5. II V I Major Chromatic Descent

Exercise 6. Left Hand Practice

Practice this next progression in your left hand only. After the first II V I, fill in the rest of the notes, using smooth voice leading.

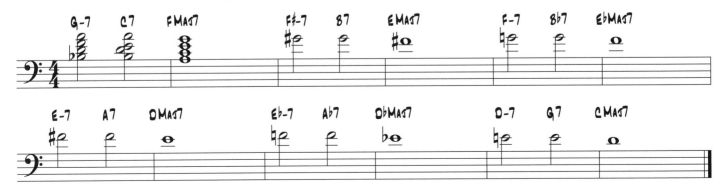

Exercise 7. II V I in Minor

Complete the next few exercises, using smooth voice leading. Note the altered tensions of these dominant chords in minor.

Exercise 8. II V I in Minor

Exercise 9. II V I in Minor

Exercise 10. II V I in Minor

Exercise 11. II V I Minor Chromatic Descent

Exercise 12. **Left Hand Practice**

Practice this next progression in your left hand only.

Exercise 13. **Comping Rhythms**

Practice playing these II V I exercises from memory, without looking at the notation.
Play each exercise once using each rhythm.

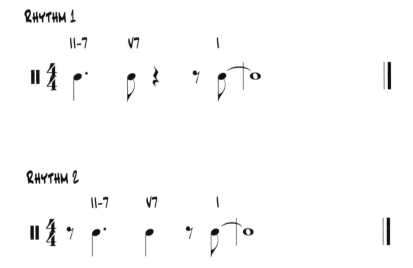

CHALLENGE

For an added challenge, set a metronome to click on beats 2 and 4, and do the exercises against that.

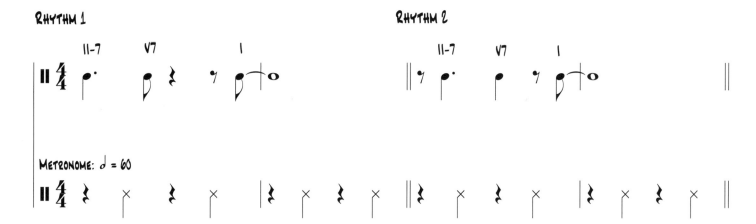

TUNES

Etude. "So Easily: Take 2"

This etude is based on the chord changes to "I Fall in Love Too Easily" by Jerome Kern. Compare this to the previous version, in chapter 1. Analyze the tension substitutions in this piece, writing the number next to the tone. Then play it through.

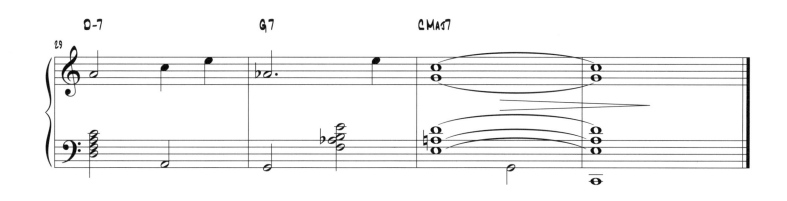

Lead Sheet. "So Easily"

Play the lead sheet to "So Easily," which was introduced in lesson 1. This time, include tensions in your voicings.

So Easily

Neil Olmstead

Etude. "I Had a Clue"

"I Had a Clue" is based upon Bill Evans' changes to the Harry Warren tune, "I Wish I Knew." This etude illustrates how chords with tensions are played against a walking bass line. In the following chapters, you will learn to create your own bass lines. The chords are comprised of *three-* and *four-note close position* voicings with tension substitutions (*9 for root* on most major and minor chords, and *13 for 5* on most dominant chords).

Most of the rhythms used here are in two-measure phrases (e.g., mm. 1–2, 7–8, etc.). This helps to eliminate rhythmic repetition. The syncopations of measures 3–6 are typical of many pianists of the bop period (1944–58). Listen to Red Garland on Miles Davis' recordings from the 1950s to hear more of this kind of rhythmic playing.

Tip

Moving the top voice *primarily by step,* in logical rhythmic phrases, helps create a strong accompaniment.

I Had a Clue

Neil Olmstead

Chord Chart. "I Had a Clue"

Create your own comping part to this tune by writing out the voicings with tension substitutions as appropriate. Move your top voice primarily by step or common tone. Give priority to the rhythmic phrasing. As discussed earlier, this type of lead sheet that shows just the chords is sometimes called a "chord chart." A blank version follows for you to write out your part.

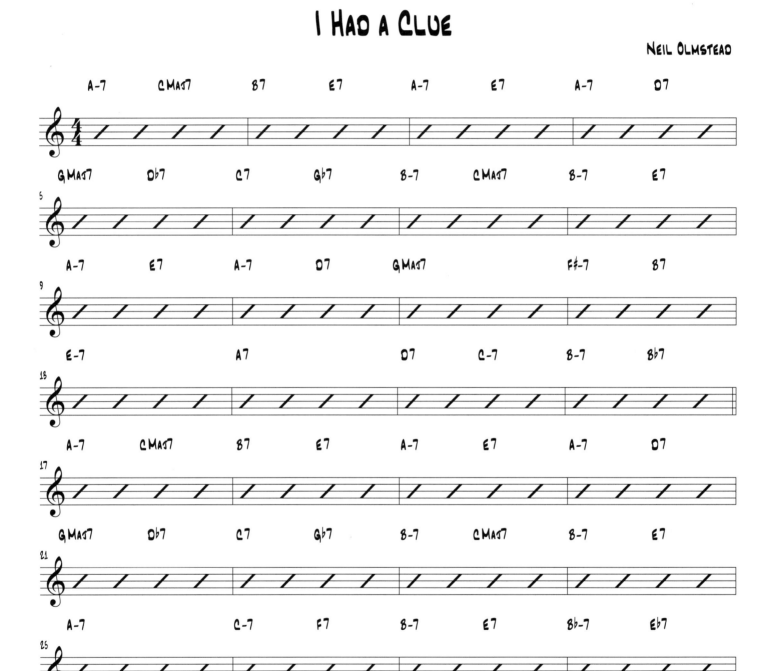

I HAD A CLUE

NEIL OLMSTEAD

I Had a Clue

Neil Olmstead

Etude. "Sweet Dolphin Suite"

"Sweet Dolphin Suite" is based on the chord changes to "Green Dolphin Street" by Kaper/Washington. This etude demonstrates a variety of left-hand voicings with tensions in different inversions. Note the smooth voice leading to the new harmonies.

SWEET DOLPHIN SUITE

Neil Olmstead

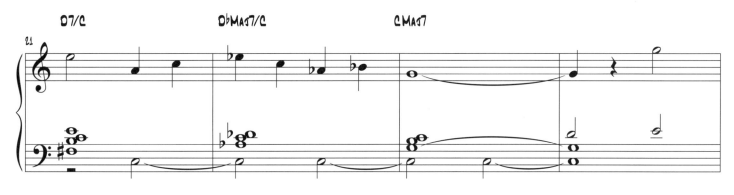

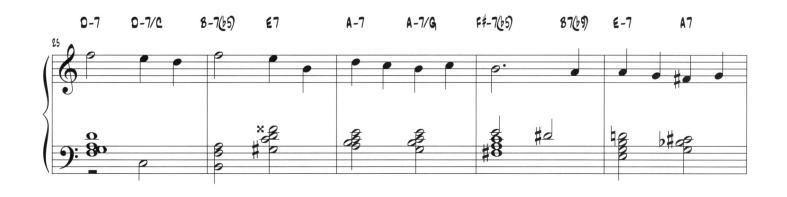

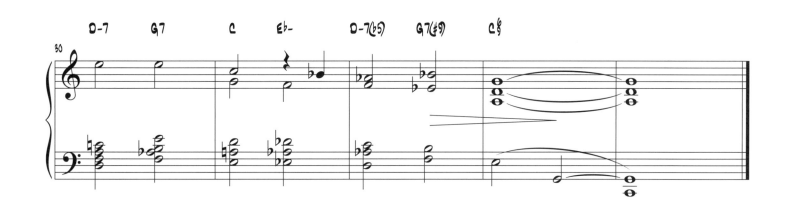

Lead Sheet. "Sweet Dolphin Suite"

Using tensions in your voicings, create your own comping part in the left hand. Voice lead smoothly to the new chords. Syncopate the melody freely and, in a medium swing groove, rhythmicize your left-hand comping.

Note that the tune ends with chords in parentheses. This point is called a *turn-around,* as the form "turns around" back to the beginning. Play these chords when you are returning to the top, but not when you are ending the tune.

PART II. Bass Lines

Now that you've reviewed the harmonic language of jazz, it's time to look at how to play bass lines in the left hand. Walking bass lines came into prominence in the 1940s. In solo and duo settings where bassists were not present, pianists have often felt inspired to play walking bass lines. Pianists such as Lennie Tristano and Dave McKenna have explored this concept deeply, and are leaders in the field. Today, solo jazz pianists often use this technique, finding it provides a subtle driving impetus to their improvisations without the weightiness of chords.

Part II explores this linear concept in a codified, graduated manner, to help you master the fundamentals of contrapuntal improvisation. These exercises and etudes will help prepare you to improvise bass lines while playing the melody, comping, and soloing.

Chapter 3. Half-Note Motives

THEORY

A common motive in cut-time and ballad (2/2) playing is the *half-note motive*. The simplest form is to have the chord root on every half note. This is used when the chord changes every two beats.

Roots Only

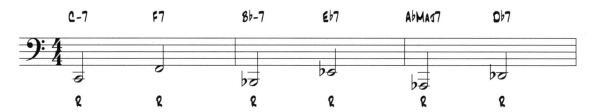

The most important and commonly used half-note motive is the *root-five,* where the root is on beat 1 and the fifth is on beat 3. It is used when the chord changes every measure.

Root-Five

When the chord changes every measure, you can also use *root-octave* or *root-five-five-root:*

Root-Octave

Root-Five-Five-Root

When the chord changes every two measures, you can use a combination of motives.

Combination

Eventually, you will use a combination of these in all circumstances. Your choice will depend on the harmonic progression and the line you wish to develop. As you become familiar with the most common motives, your flexibility at improvising alternate motives will increase.

Tips

1. Keep your left-hand line basic so that it offers strong support for your right hand. Remember, it is an accompaniment to an improvisation.

2. Become fluent on the root-five motive. It is used most often, and learning it will help you learn the others.

PRACTICE

Bass Line Practice

The bass lines in the following exercises are built primarily from the different kinds of half-note motives. Practice each line until you can play it easily.

1. Practice each bass line by itself.

2. Add the right-hand comping part.

Exercise 1. Roots Only

Exercise 2. Root-Five

Exercise 3. Root-Octave

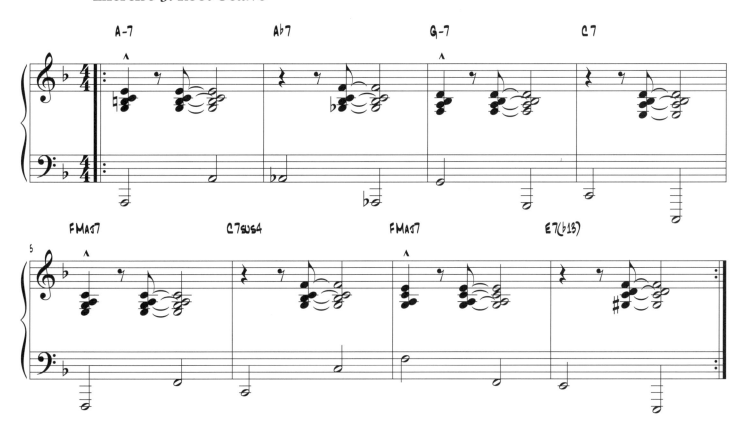

Exercise 4. Root-Five-Five-Root

Exercise 5. Combination

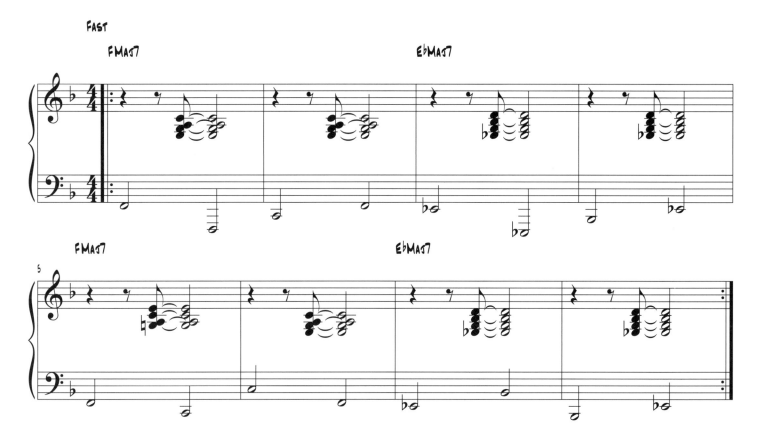

Comping Practice

Create your own right-hand comping part over each set of chord changes (see chapters 1 and 2). Practice them along with the given bass lines. Focus on voice leading and rhythmic drive. Try different tempos.

Exercise 1. Comping: Roots Only

Exercise 2. Comping: Root-Five

Exercise 3. Comping: Root-Octave

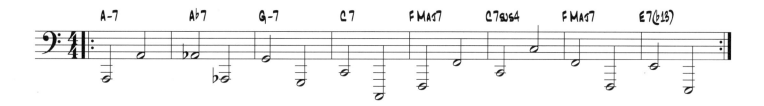

Exercise 4. Comping: Root-Five-Five-Root

Exercise 5. Comping: Combination

Arrow Sheet: "A Night At Play"

Create your own half-note motive bass line to the tune "A Night At Play" using the arrow sheet as a guide. Your primary goal is to play the chord root on the first beat of each chord. Play the appropriate root or fifth, depending on the melodic direction of the arrow.

The arrow sheet looks like this:

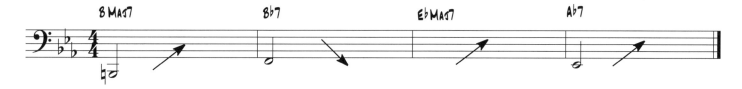

Your completed bass line should look something like this:

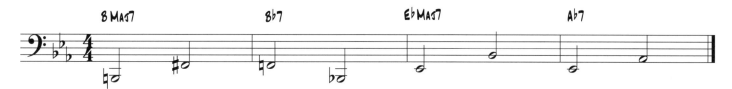

Try to create a smooth line. When you are done, compare the line you created to the written bass line in the etude, "A Night At Play." They should be similar, or even exactly the same. Notice the use of the various half-note motives shown at the beginning of this chapter.

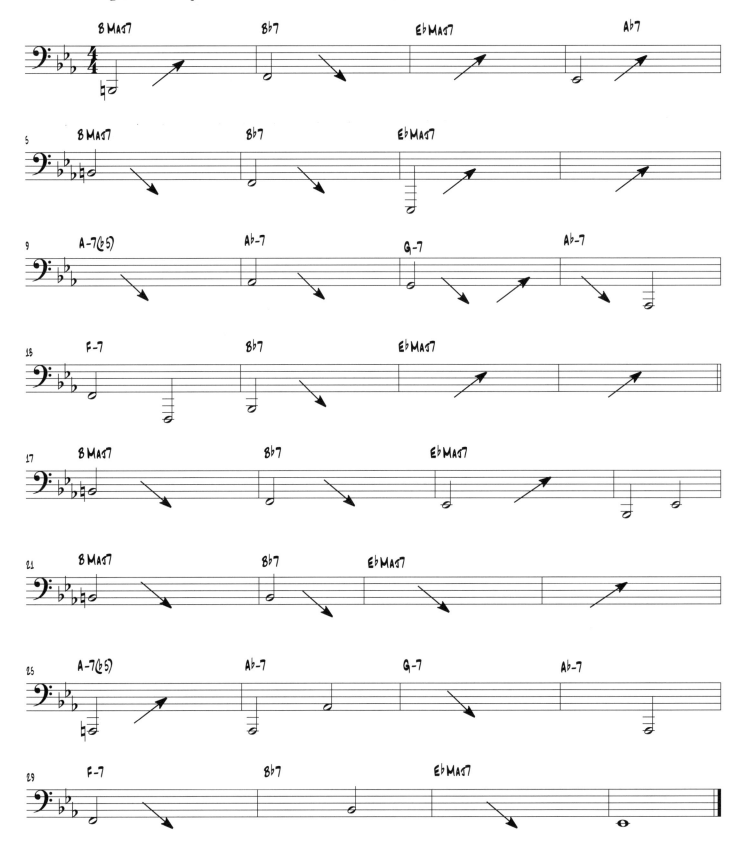

TUNES

Etude. "A Night At Play"

"A Night At Play" is based on the chord changes to the Cole Porter tune "Night and Day." It illustrates the half-note motive as used in a ballad feel (2/2).

Play this tune with deep legato and straight eighth notes, thus rendering a *two* feel. After playing it straight, play it again, swinging the eighth notes in the last eight measures. You'll find the pulse naturally gravitating toward a *four* feel at the end.

Note the three-part texture is interspersed throughout this tune (e.g., mm. 6–9). A slow tempo augmented by a *third voice* below the melody, or harmonized with right-hand voicings, is usually richer and more convincingly ballad-like. Also, note the range and contour of the bass line. What are its highest and lowest notes?

These techniques should be used in your own arrangements.

A Night At Play

Neil Olmstead

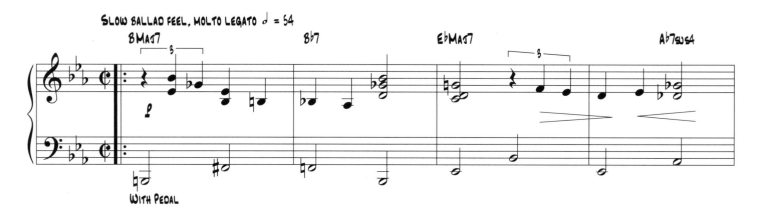

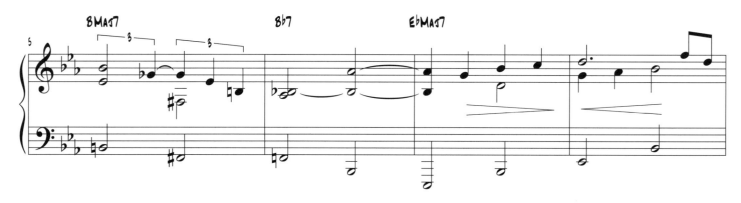

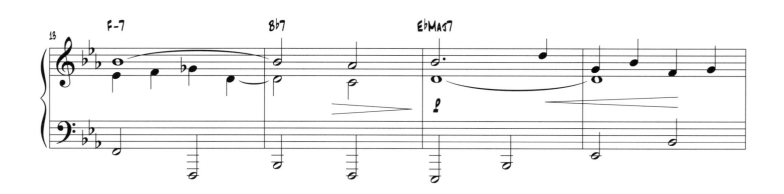

Lead Sheet. "A Night At Play"

Create your own arrangement to "A Night At Play." Use the CD as a reference.

1. Use each type of half-note motive as frequently as possible throughout two choruses of the tune. Then play another chorus, and improvise a bass line that combines these motives.

2. Play the tune as a ballad (2/2), using straight eighths in the right hand. Then play it as a swing (4/4) tune, syncopating the melody and swinging the eighths.

A Night At Play

Neil Olmstead

Chapter 4. Ballad to Swing

Moving from a half-time feel to a quarter-time feel

THEORY

As we've seen in the previous chapter, half-note bass lines are generally expressed in two time feels: ballad and swing.

Ballad or "half-time" feel is characterized by a rhythm of two beats in the measure, strongly rooted in beats 1 and 3. To attain this feel, use long tones, straight eighth notes, and quarter-note triplets in your right hand. Avoid swinging eighth notes. Quarter-note triplets are very helpful in establishing this feel, especially if the ballad feel is being approached from a swing feel.

Swing or "quarter time" feel is characterized by a rhythm of four beats in the measure, with accents on beats 2 and 4. A swing feel can easily move to a walking bass line. To attain a swing feel, give your eighth notes a lilting swing. The feel will naturally gravitate toward a subtle accent on beats 2 and 4.

Shifting from one feel to another usually occurs after a groove has been fully established. Sometimes, 32 measures or more of ballad will then give way to swing. "Flora," on page 50, illustrates this in measure 16, when the shift from ballad to swing occurs.

PRACTICE

Shifting Time Feels

These short examples will give you practice modulating between ballad and swing. In actual song arrangements, these shifts generally occur over longer musical sections—16 or 32 measures, or even several choruses.

Each exercise begins as a ballad and then shifts to swing. At first, play them without following the written repeats.

1. First, practice the right hand by itself. Notice the change of rhythms when it shifts to swing. Play the eighth notes straight in the ballad sections, but with a swing feel in the swing sections.

2. With your left hand, add a bass line of half-note motives.

3. Practice each exercise until you are comfortable shifting between the two feels.

Exercise 1. Shifting Time Feels

Exercise 2. Shifting Time Feels

Exercise 3. Shifting Time Feels

CHALLENGE

When you are comfortable moving from ballad to swing, play each exercise again, but observe the repeats so that you can practice moving from swing to ballad.

Arrow Sheet: "Cabernet"

Play the arrow sheet based on "Cabernet" using half-note motives. Follow the direction of the arrow when playing the missing half notes. Practice this until you can play it easily. Then add a comping part in your right hand. Check your bass line against the etude to "Cabernet." They should be similar.

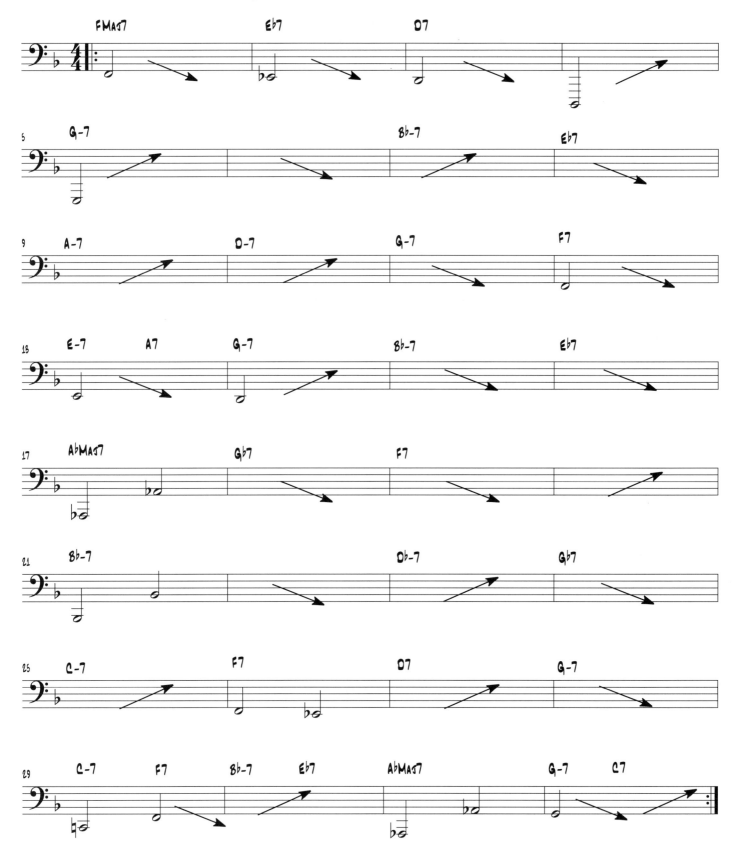

TUNES

Etude. "Flora"

This etude, based on the chord changes to Johnny Mercer's standard "Laura," moves from ballad to swing with a constant half-note motive in the left hand. The modulation from ballad to swing is much more typical of what you will find in actual arrangements. The shift occurs only after the ballad groove is fully established. Play it as written until you are comfortable with the two time feels. Then, for an added challenge, play it reading the bass line and chord symbols, but improvising the right hand. Shift freely between the two time feels.

Flora

Neil Olmstead

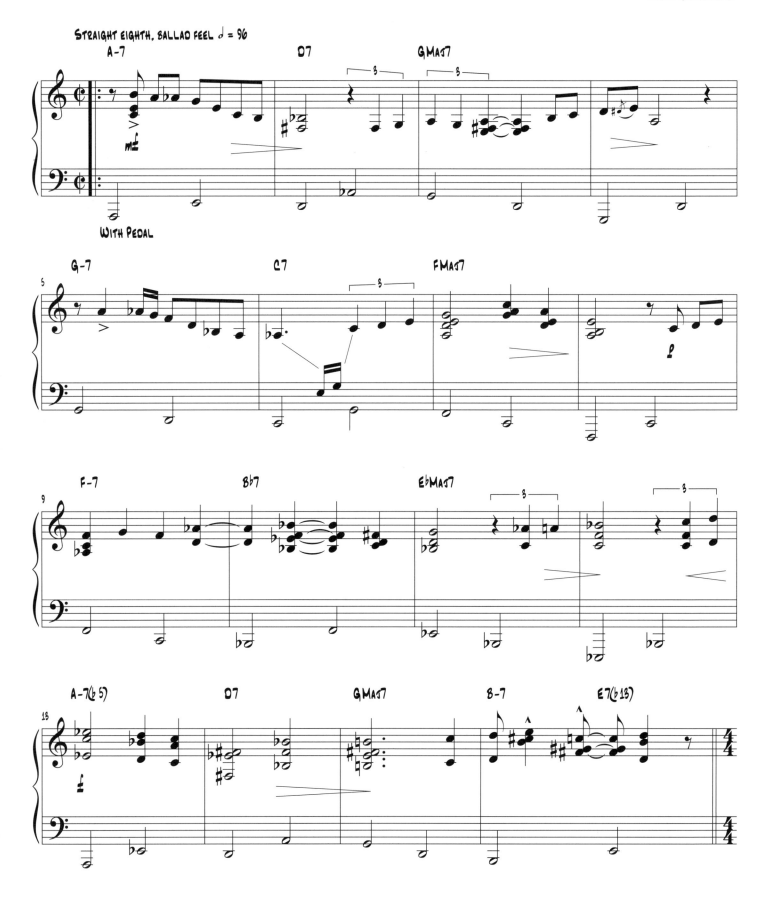

> **Tip**
>
> When learning any tunes, practice two feels: ballads as swing tunes and swing tunes as ballads. Then practice moving from one feel to the other.

Etude. "Cabernet"

This piece, based on the chord changes to Henry Mancini's tune "The Days of Wine and Roses," is an example of an improvisation that moves between swing and ballad feels. Note that the straight eighth notes and the quarter-note triplets help to slow the groove for the ballad feel. Then note how easy it is to get back to the "four" feel by simply swinging the phrase group of the last two bars. Practice this etude until you are comfortable with these rhythmic shifts.

CABERNET

NEIL OLMSTEAD

Lead Sheet. "Cabernet"

Practice "Cabernet" from the lead sheet, using it to create your own bass line and comping part. Note the tonal modulation in the middle of the tune. In the 1979 recording session of Bill Evans' CD *Affinity,* Toots Thielemans introduced an arrangement of "The Days of Wine and Roses" that included this modulation.

Chapter 5. Walking Bass
Moving from a half-note motive to a quarter-note motive

THEORY

As we've seen, a quarter-time feel can be expressed with a half-note bass in the left hand. However, the quarter-note *walking bass* is the ultimate resolution of this implied rhythm.

The same root-five motive can be expressed in half notes or quarter notes.

Additionally, you can approach a new root chromatically–from above with an *upper* chromatic approach or from below with a *lower* chromatic approach.

When the harmonic rhythm is four beats per chord, roots, fifths, octaves, and chromatic approaches may be combined freely.

PRACTICE

Walking Exercise

Play a walking bass line using the new material: root-five, root-chromatic, and root-octave.

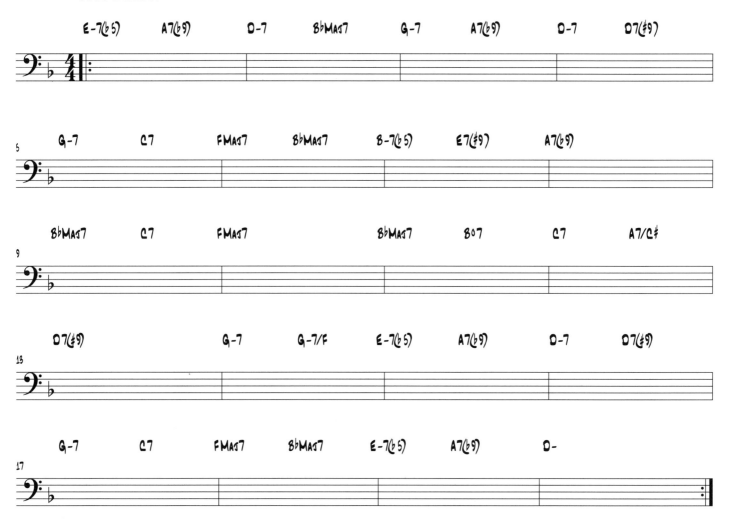

Arrow Sheet: "I Remember Soo"

Using the arrows as a guide to playing the missing quarter notes, complete the bass line to "I Remember Soo." Practice this until you can play it easily. Then add a comping part in your right hand. Check your bass line against the etude to "I Remember Soo," later this chapter. They should be similar, starting at measure 17 of the etude.

TUNES

Etude. "I Remember Soo"

This piece, based on the chord changes to the Mercer/Schertzinger standard "I Remember You," starts with a mix of half notes and quarter notes, then settles into a steady walking groove. Practice it in an easy swing feel.

Focus on balance and tone between your hands. An active bass line that is too loud can easily become overpowering.

I Remember Soo

Neil Olmstead

Lead Sheet. "I Remember Soo"

Practice "I Remember Soo" from the lead sheet, using half notes, quarter notes, and chromatic approach notes in your bass line.

I Remember Soo

Neil Olmstead

Etude. "How Deep Is Emotion"

Based on the chord changes to "How Deep Is the Ocean" by Irving Berlin, the bass line in this piece moves along rather energetically using half notes, quarter notes, and chromatic approaches, as well as root-octave motives. At faster tempos, a simple root-five motive will provide a strong accompaniment to more complex linear improvisations.

HOW DEEP IS EMOTION

NEIL OLMSTEAD

Lead Sheet. "How Deep Is Emotion"

Time feels can be used to create an organic flow of temporal development in an arrangement. They can encourage a natural development of a solo, and of the overall form of the piece.

To review, we have studied three time feels so far:

Half   Half-time or "ballad" feel. Half notes in the left hand; straight eighths, long tones, and quarter-note triplets in the right hand.

Quarter   Quarter-time or "swing" feel. Quarter notes in the left hand; swing eighths in the right hand

Quarter/Half   Quarter-over-half-time feel. Half notes in the left hand; swing eighths in the right hand.

Here is how two common song forms (AABA and ABAC) might be arranged, using quarter-time, half-time, and quarter-over-half-time (quarter/half) feels.

AABA

Practice AABA tunes like this:

Head: AA	BA	Solo: AABA	Head: AA	BA	End
Half	Quarter/Half	Quarter	Quarter	Quarter/Half	Half

ABAC

Practice ABAC tunes like this:

Head: A	B	AC	Solo: AB	AC, AB, Head: A	C	End
Half	Quarter/Half	Quarter	Quarter/Half	Quarter	Quarter/Half	Half

In your own arrangements, use this variety in your time feels.

> **Tip**
>
> Beginning slowly is generally more effective than ending slowly. A ballad feel at the beginning is likely to work, but a ballad feel at the end may be too long and difficult to play effectively.

Using all of the techniques we have studied so far (see "Critical Tools" at the end of this chapter), arrange the lead sheet to "How Deep Is Emotion" using the ABAC arrangement above. Play several choruses, first comping in the right hand and then improvising a solo.

HOW DEEP IS EMOTION

NEIL OLMSTEAD

Critical Tools

Use all of the techniques we have studied so far to create new interpretations of tunes in your repertoire.

Bass-Line Motives

1. Root-five

2. Root-octave

3. Root-chromatic approach

Time Feels

1. Half-note ballad

2. Half-note swing

3. Quarter-note swing

4. Temporal development

Textures

1. Two lines

2. Right-hand chord, left-hand line

3. Right-hand line with third voice, left-hand line

Chapter 6. Linear Motives

Ascending and descending stepwise and scalar motives for bass lines

THEORY

Ascending and descending stepwise motives lie at the heart of contrapuntal improvisation. Used alongside the root-five motive combinations, they energize the music with a focused directional quality.

Linear motives are used to connect the roots of chords that are a fourth apart, such as in II-V progressions. They contain a double chromatic approach to the root of the next chord. This chromatic approach is characteristic of bebop.

On minor chords, the added chromatic note is the major third of the chord. On major chords, the chromatic is the minor third. On minor 7 (♭5) and on dominant 7 (♭9), the second pitch can be lowered by a half step.

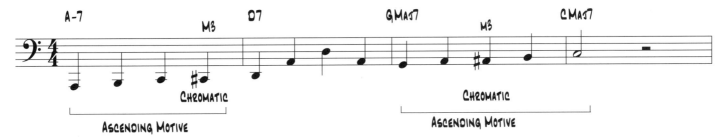

The *descending stepwise motive* connects two roots a fourth apart by descending five notes of a scale (in 4/4 time). The scale or mode used will vary depending on the chords being connected (commonly, Mixolydian for dominant chords, Dorian for minor chords, and Ionian for major chords, but altered dominant scales, Locrian, Phrygian, and others are also possible). Descending motives generally give a sense of resolution.

PRACTICE

Comping Study 1: Flying Towers

Comping Study 1 includes stepwise motives exclusively. In performance practice, you should generally use a *combination* of stepwise, root-five, and scalar motives (discussed later in this lesson).

1. Practice the study as written until you can play it easily.

2. Practice reading the chord symbols only, but improvising your own left-hand bass line that consists primarily of stepwise motives. Play many choruses, until you are comfortable improvising this kind of bass line.

Arrow Sheet: "Flying Towers"

Complete the arrow sheet based on the chord changes to "My Shining Hour" by Johnny Mercer. Play the root at the beginning of each new chord, and then continue in the indicated direction, primarily using stepwise motives. Practice the bass line alone until you can play it easily. Then add a comping part in your right hand. Check your work against Comping Study 2, which follows this exercise. They should be similar.

Comping Study 2: Flying Towers

Read the given bass line, and improvise your own right-hand comping part using the voicings shown, but your own syncopated rhythm. If you played exactly what was indicated in the previous exercise, you would have played this bass line. Try creating your own bass line with a syncopated comping part. Use a combination of stepwise, scalar, and root-five motives.

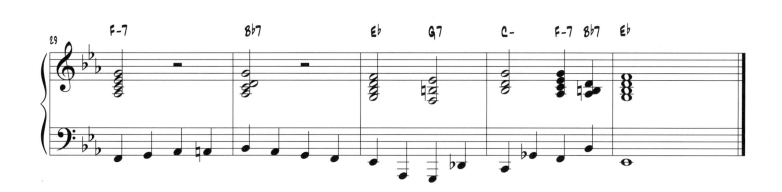

THEORY

Scalar Motives

Ascending and descending *scalar* motives–featuring an entire eight-note scale–can be used when a chord is held for two or more measures.

Ascending

Descending

When two measures of the same chord continue with another chord of the same root, a chromatic addition to the scale will let you sound the root again in bar 3. Place a chromatic so that the chord tones sound on strong beats (beats 1 and 3).

The note that is chromaticized will depend on the chord and direction of the line. When descending or ascending on a *dominant* chord, use a chromatic *seventh*.

Ascending

Descending

When ascending on a minor or major chord, use a chromatic 7.

Ascending Minor

Ascending Major

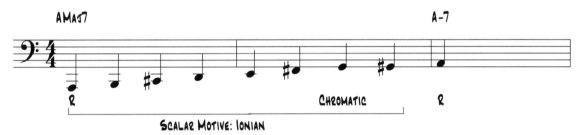

When descending on a minor or major chord, use a chromatic 6.

Descending Minor

Descending Major

For practice using scales in right-hand soloing, see appendix D, "Linear Independence Exercises."

PRACTICE

Comping Study 3: "You Are in Flight with the Music"

This piece, based on the chord changes to the Dietz/Schwartz tune "You and the Night and the Music," illustrates the use of scalewise motives and chromatics. Practice the bass line until you can play it easily. Then add your own comping part. Finally, create your own bass line to go along with it. Use primarily stepwise and scalar motives.

You Are in Flight with the Music

Neil Olmstead

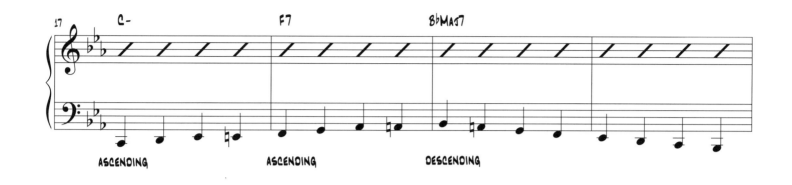

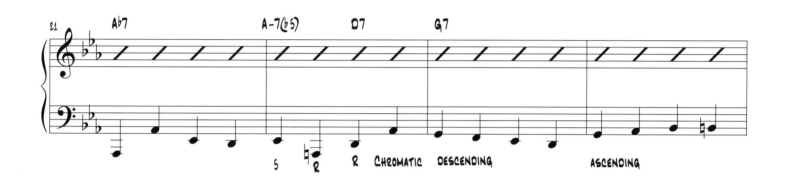

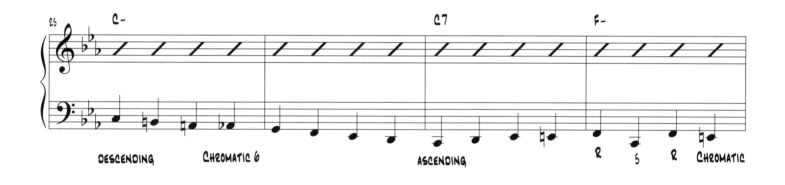

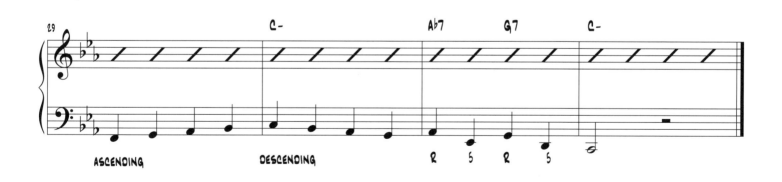

Study Both Directions

Practice long arching lines that ascend as far as the range allows (G3) and then descend as low as the piano allows (A1). Using a large range in the bass line sounds especially attractive, and it is a good habit to develop. This will allow you to be more melodic in your lower voice, particularly when you are resting in the upper voice.

Tip: Use Your Thumb

Practice crossing your thumb under regularly, so that you will not "run out" of fingers. This habit will provide you with the flexibility of having the fingers necessary to go as far as you'd like in either direction.

For a good left-hand finger-flexibility exercise, practice bass lines with the following finger combinations:

123

134

13

135

A second exercise: Try those fingerings with improvised right-hand lines. Yes, it's a bit tricky, but you'll enjoy the freedom of all those fingers, with additional thumb flexibility.

TUNES

Etude. "Dove Feathers"

This piece, based on the chord changes to the Victor Young tune "Love Letters," illustrates a combination of the many different motive types studied so far.

- The bass line in measures 1–2 might, at first glance, appear to be a descending scale. However, since the chord changes at measure 2, and each chord must be supported individually, it is better to look at the bass line as two adjacent stepwise motives.

- Measures 3–4 are similarly two adjacent ascending motives.

- Measure 5 is a root-five and root-chromatic followed by an ascending motive in measure 6.

- In measure 7, a slight departure from the motives appears, where an ascending line to the third is followed by a chromatic approach to the root.

Analyze the rest of the left hand part for motives and possible departures from the motives. Then practice the etude until you can play it comfortably.

Dove Feathers

Neil Olmstead

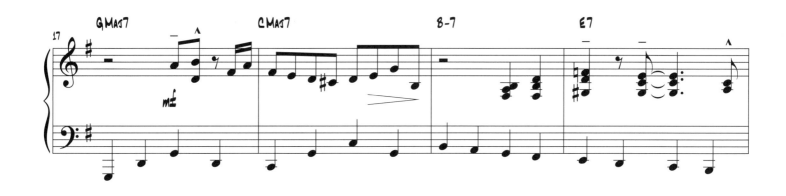

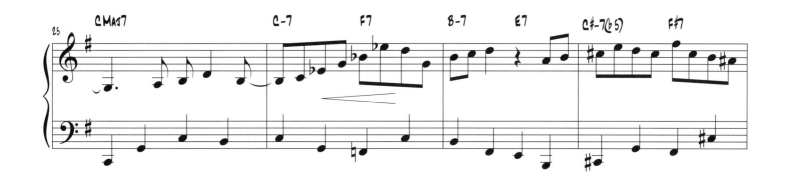

Lead Sheet. "Dove Feathers"

Practice "Dove Feathers" from the lead sheet, using all the various motives you have studied so far to create your own arrangement.

DOVE FEATHERS

NEIL OLMSTEAD

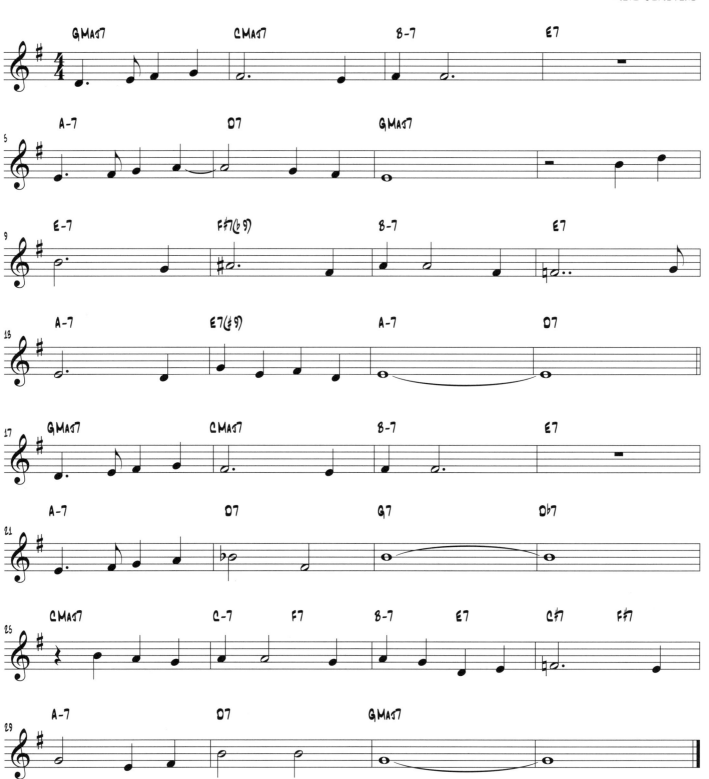

Lead Sheet. "Winds of Kyle"

"Winds of Kyle" is based on the chord changes to the Ralph Rainger standard "If I Should Lose You." Practice the melody, solo, and comping while using all the various bass motives you have studied so far. Listen to the CD for possible variations in the bass line.

Motives Studied So Far

Root-five motives

Root-chromatic motives

Ascending stepwise motive

Descending stepwise motive

Ascending and descending scalar motives

Winds of Kyle

Neil Olmstead

How to Practice Playing from Lead Sheets

Try this practice approach on this lead sheet and on any other tunes where you are using a walking bass.

Practice the Head

1. Practice the melody in the right hand and roots only in the left hand.

2. Comp chords in the right hand against roots only in the left hand.

3. Comp chords in the right hand with walking bass and mixed rhythms in the left hand.

4. Play the melody in the right hand with walking bass and mixed rhythms in the left hand.

Practice Soloing

1. Solo in the right hand against roots only in the left hand.

2. Solo in the right hand against a walking bass and mixed rhythms in the left hand.

3. Solo in the right hand against a walking bass in the left hand.

Chapter 7. The Jazz Waltz
Triple Meter Bass Lines

THEORY

The *ascending stepwise* motive in 3/4 is similar to the 4/4 version, though it does not require the chromatic. To ascend a fourth, follow the scale suggested by the chords.

To descend a fifth, you can use the root-five motive.

The *root-five-chromatic* figure can be used to ascend or descend.

Ascending

Descending

> **Tip**
>
> Although a lower chromatic may be a chord tone, as in the D7 (ascending) and D7 (descending) measures in the preceding examples, thinking of them as chromatic approaches will help you maintain your sense of the motive's linearity. Using linear motives primarily, rather than just arpeggios, will give your bass lines a sense of forward momentum.

To further emphasize the root, repeat the root on beat 3 with a lower chromatic on beat 2 (as illustrated in mm. 1 and 3 below).

To superimpose a *two feel,* play the root-five motive in dotted quarter notes.

Mixed rhythms of half notes, quarter notes, and occasionally eighth notes may be combined freely with root-five motivic material. This excerpt is from "Spring Cardinal" (mm. 13 to 16), which you will learn later in this chapter.

PRACTICE

Arrow Sheet: "Triple"

Create your own bass line to "Triple" using the arrow sheet as a guide. Practice the bass line alone until you can play it easily. Then add a comping part in your right hand. Check your bass line against "Comping: Triple" that follows this arrow sheet. They should be similar.

Comping: Triple

Analyze the types of 3/4 motives used in this comping exercise. Practice it exactly as written. Then practice its written bass line along with your own chord voicings, based on the chord symbols. Finally, play your own chord voicings and your own bass line using the 3/4 motives discussed in this chapter.

TUNES

Etude. "Spring Cardinal"

This tune is based on the chord changes to "Up with the Lark," by Jerome Kern. Although a jazz waltz feel is apparent, the bass voice opens with mixed rhythms (mm. 1–22). The rhythm then develops toward a steady quarter-note bass, appearing in measure 23. As this example illustrates, a strong jazz waltz feel can be created using a walking bass line based predominantly on root-five motives. The chromatic approaches help strengthen this feel.

The open time feel in combination with the root-five motives allow more liberal use of the damper pedal than would a more stepwise walking line. Notice how the augmented fifths in measures 43–46 add an interesting whole-tone quality to the harmony.

SPRING CARDINAL

NEIL OLMSTEAD

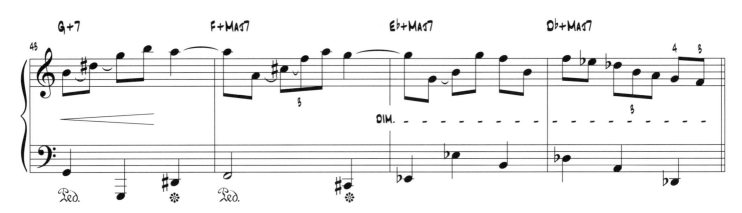

Lead Sheet. "Spring Cardinal"

Using all of the 3/4 bass line motives we have studied so far, practice the lead sheet to "Spring Cardinal." Play several choruses, first comping in the right hand and then improvising a solo. Try creating a slow rhythmic development in your own bass line.

Spring Cardinal

Neil Olmstead

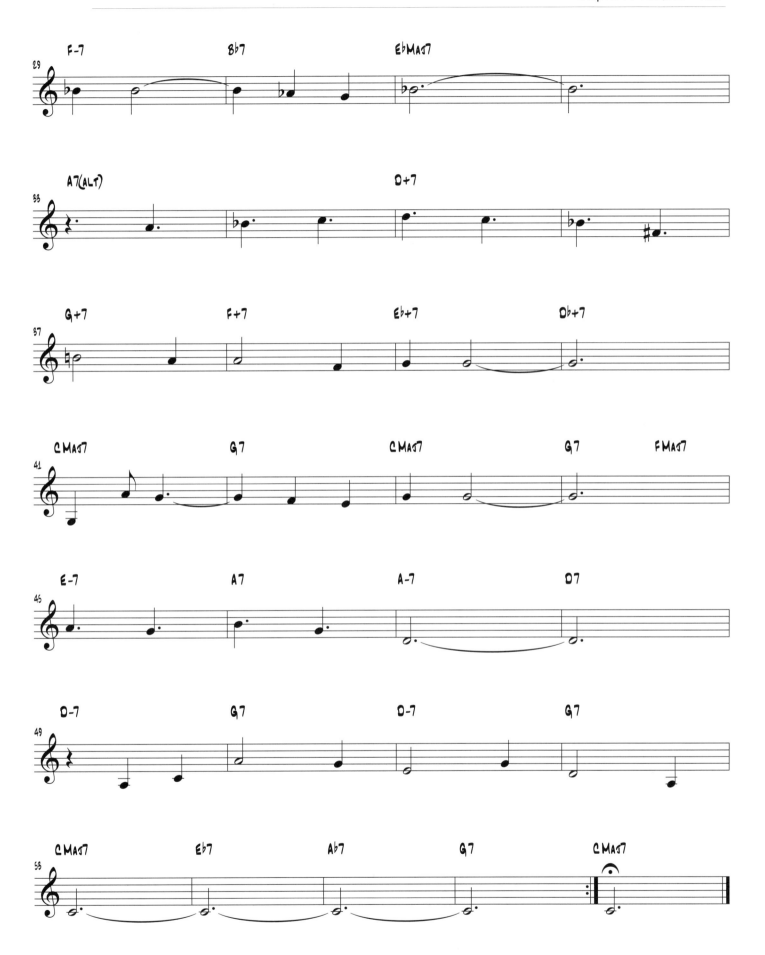

Etude. "Summer Flight"

This tune is based on the chord changes to the Harry Warren standard, "Summer Night." It opens up with mixed rhythms of root-five motivic material, before settling into a walking groove. When two chords appear in one measure (mm. 36–38), you can place the second chord either on the "and" of beat 2 (m. 37) or directly on beat 3 (m. 38).

In measure 57, consider the F-sharp on the D–7(♭5) as a chromatic approach to the G7 root, rather than as a major third on a minor chord.

SUMMER FLIGHT

NEIL OLMSTEAD

Lead Sheet. "Summer Flight"

Using 3/4 bass line motives, arrange the lead sheet to "Summer Flight." Play several choruses, first comping in the right hand and then improvising a solo.

Chapter 8. Compound Bass Lines

Inversions and Line Clichés

THEORY

A *compound bass line* implies two voices within the same bass line. Compound bass lines exist in chord progressions with inverted chords and line clichés.

Inversions

An *inverted* chord has a bass note other than the chord root. The chord symbol "C-7/B♭" means a C minor 7 chord sounds with a B-flat in the bass. When you create a bass line that includes inverted chords, play the indicated bass note first. Then play either the fifth or third of the chord. This combination implies two voices in one, hence a compound line.

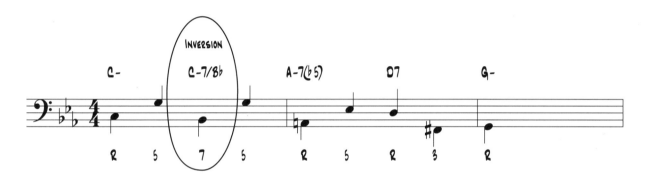

PRACTICE

Inversions

Practice the following progression. At each chord symbol, the chord root or the indicated bass note is always played first. Then the root, fifth, or third is chosen to support the strongest linear motion. This is how the compound line is created.

Notice the repeated notes in measures 13 to 14. Repeated notes, in a descending pattern, are always a strong bass line.

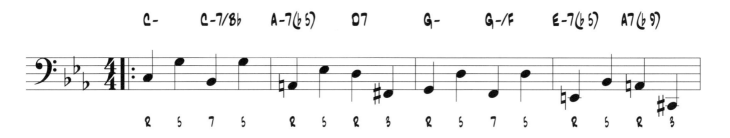

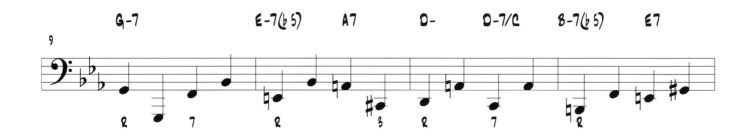

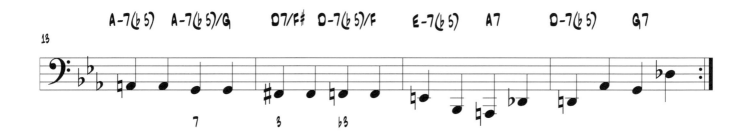

THEORY

Line Clichés

A *line cliché* is a stepwise descending or ascending line played against a single stationary note. This can imply a compound line; the stationary note is one voice, the moving line is the other voice.

The moving line may be in the upper or lower voice. Line clichés may be written as inversions, as discussed previously, or as extensions, as in the following example.

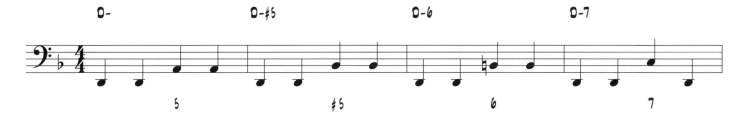

PRACTICE

Line Clichés

Practice this progression. What are the different line clichés? What compound lines do they create? Practice the bass line alone until you can play it easily. Then add a comping part in your right hand.

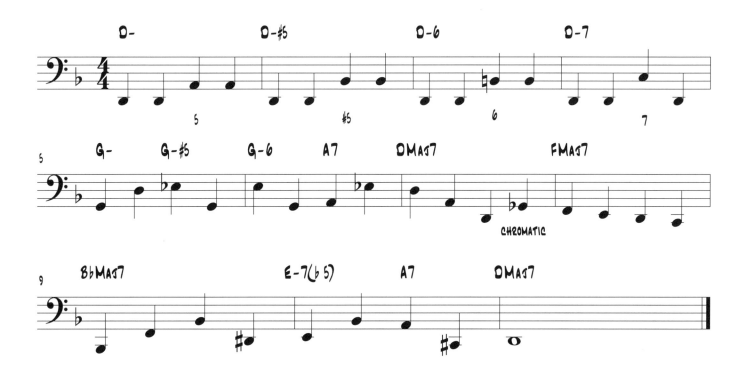

TUNES

Etude. "Golden Feelings"

This tune is based on the chord changes to "Golden Earrings" by Victor Young. The first two measures contain a descending bass line that includes inversions of C minor. You can play the bass line to this two-measure progression in a variety of ways. Compare the following measures, which all contain the same descending progression: measures 1–2, 9–10, 25–26, 33–34, 41–42, and 57–58.

Practice the left hand to these measures while comping in the right hand. This will give you some experience in handling these common inversions.

While you practice this tune, consider these questions:

- How do you analyze the bass line in measure 5?

- Why is there a chromatic in the bass of measure 51?

GOLDEN FEELINGS

NEIL OLMSTEAD

Lead Sheet. "Golden Feelings"

Observe the inversions while playing the bass line in "Golden Feelings." Work out the melody, and then play several choruses, first comping and then improvising a solo.

GOLDEN FEELINGS

Neil Olmstead

Lead Sheet. "Wild Bill"

10

This tune is based on the chord changes to the standard "Like Someone in Love" by Jimmy Van Heusen. It contains many inversions. Other tunes to check out for inversions and line clichés include Benny Golson's "Whisper Not" and John Carisi's "Israel."

WILD BILL

NEIL OLMSTEAD

Chapter 9. Embellishing the Bass Line
Kicks and Triplets

THEORY

Embellishing a line with eighth notes is common practice among bassists. This gives the bass line a rhythmic "kick."

Pianists most often use embellishing motives when they are accompanying soloists or between their own solo phrases. Embellishing notes have a swing feel, and are sometimes a complete triplet. In 4/4, these motives most often occur on beats 1 and 3, serving as embellishments to beats 2 and 4. Embellishing motives can also be effective on beats 2 and 4. Embellishing motives are rhythmically most effective when they are comprised of wide intervals. The following embellishing motives are listed in order of how common they are and how easy they are to play.

1. **Returning Note.** Come back to the first note of an ascending or descending stepwise motive.

2. **Repeated Note.** Play the same note again, generally with alternating fingers (e.g., 3-1 or 2-1).

3. **Octave/Fifth Kick.** Play the chord's root or fifth at the octave.

4. **Octave Thirds.** Play the chord's third an octave below the line. This adds strong harmonic motion to a circle-of-fifths progression.

113

5. Triplet Motives. These sound best when constructed of fourths, but they may also be constructed of triads. Avoid stepwise or chromatic triplets.

- *Anticipated Triplet.* Start the embellishing motive with the root of the upcoming chord. This can be with or without the octave drop. Note the fingerings.

- *Anticipated Without Octave.* Here's the same example but without the octave drop. Note the fingerings.

- *Right-Hand Coordinated Triplet.* Play a chord voicing in the right hand on the downbeat. Follow the chord with the left hand playing the root and fifth in the bass. This is surprisingly easy to master, and it sounds very strong.

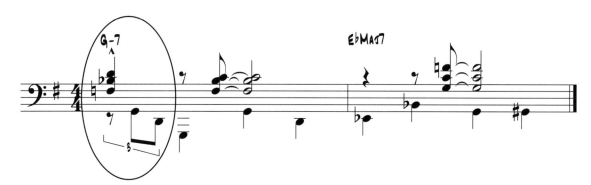

- *Consecutive Triplet.* Play two triplet motives over two octaves.

Eighth notes in the bass should *not* be used to simply "fill" the line in a stepwise manner as in the following example:

PRACTICE

Embellished Motive

Practice each embellishment exercise until your hands are comfortable with the shapes and your groove is secure. Comp in the right hand.

Exercise 1. Returning Notes

Exercise 2. Repeating Notes

Exercise 3. Octave Kick

Exercise 4. Octave Thirds

Exercise 5. Triplet Motive

Exercise 6. Anticipated Triplet Motive

Exercise 7. Right Hand Coordinated Triplet Motive

Combined Embellishments Exercise

Practice this 16-measure bass line. This exercise contains many types of embellishments—more than you'd play in an actual tune. Practice the bass line alone until you are comfortable with the rhythmic feel of the embellishing motives. What motives can you identify? See the analysis following this exercise.

> **Motives Used**
>
> Measure 1: Right-hand coordinated triplet
>
> Measure 2 and 3: Returning note
>
> Measure 4 and 14: Anticipated triplet
>
> Measure 5 and 13: Fifth
>
> Measure 6, 8, 12, and 16: Repeated note
>
> Measure 7, 11, and 14: Octave/fifth kick
>
> Measure 10: Consecutive triplet

TUNES

Etude. "Go For It!"

This tune is based on the chord changes to "Nice Work If You Can Get It," by George Gershwin. It highlights the octave-third motive, which first occurs in measures 1 to 3. This motive adds strong harmonic implications to the bass line. It is typically used in "cycle-five" motion. The right-hand coordinated motive occurs in measure 17. The octave-kick motive occurs in measure 20.

Etude. "Freezing Fog"

This tune is inspired by "Funk in Deep Freeze," by Hank Mobley. The right hand begins with a comping texture (mm. 1–8) and then moves to a linear texture. The right-hand coordinated triplets in measures 2 and 11 are easy to play, and particularly effective in this comping texture.

Note that the right hand rarely plays eighth notes along with the left hand. For example, measure 2 has left-hand eighth notes on beat 2 and a triplet on beat 3, and the right hand plays off beat 1 and on beat 3. Unison eighth notes between the hands, as in measure 25, are rare.

FREEZING FOG

NEIL OLMSTEAD

Lead Sheet. "Freezing Fog"

Use the lead sheet to create your arrangement of "Freezing Fog." Include a variety of embellishing motives in your bass line.

FREEZING FOG

NEIL OLMSTEAD

Lead Sheet. "In Her Sleek Way"

11 This example is based on the chord changes to Dave Brubeck's "In Your Own Sweet Way." The vamp is a prime spot for using embellishment.

In Her Sleek Way

NEIL OLMSTEAD

Chapter 10. Pedal Point

THEORY

A *pedal point* is a sustained bass note, generally set under changing harmonies. Pedal points are usually on the dominant or tonic note of the key. They are particularly effective at *turnarounds*—chord progressions that prepare for a repeat of a tune or a section of a tune (as in first endings).

The two most common types of pedal points are *tonic* and *dominant*. In a *tonic pedal point,* the tonic of the key is held or repeated. In a *dominant pedal point,* the dominant note is sustained.

Octave displacement of a pedal point (tonic or dominant) is when you repeat a pedal note up or down an octave. This adds to the music's rhythmic drive. It can also be easier to play than a single repeated note.

You can also add a fifth between your octaves. This technique can be used to displace the rhythm, giving a secondary sense of 3/4. This is called *rhythmic displacement.* It adds an interesting "tertial" (three feel) effect over the binary (two feel) rhythm.

A dominant pedal may be *chromatically enhanced* with upper and lower neighbor tones. Lennie Tristano used this effect frequently, as we will see later in this book.

To use pedal points effectively, begin by analyzing the different tonal areas in the tune. Key areas change frequently in jazz, so you should identify these regions first. Some tunes, such as "Autumn Leaves," move only from major to relative minor. Others, such as "All The Things You Are," have many different key areas. Identifying these areas will help you to find an effective place to apply pedal point. Remember, they are particularly effective at turnarounds.

As tonal areas change, the pedal point can also change. This is effective when *linking pedals* in stepwise motion. With this technique, the pedal moves by incremental step. In the example below, as the tonal area descends, the dominant pedal also descends in similar chromatic motion.

Embellishing motives may be used with pedal points. They generally occur at the end of a pedal point or within the pedal point, as illustrated. The following examples are of displaced dominant pedals with embellishments.

Ending the Pedal (Triplet)

Within the Pedal (Kick)

Within the Pedal (Triplet)

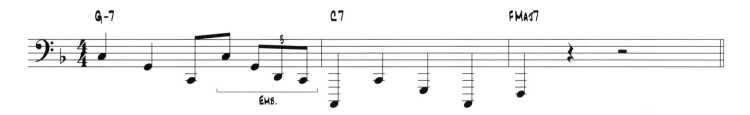

PRACTICE

Pedal Point Exercises

Practice each example until you are comfortable with the sound and groove of each type of pedal point.

Exercise 1. Tonic and Dominant Pedals

Tip

When you repeat a note, alternating your fingers will help you achieve a more legato articulation.

Exercise 2. Octave Displacement

Exercise 3. Rhythmic Displacement

Exercise 4. Chromatically Enhanced

Exercise 5. Linking Pedals

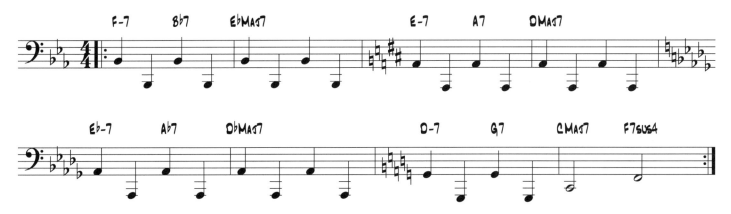

Exercise 6. Embellishment

Exercise 7. Embellishment

Exercise 8. Embellishment

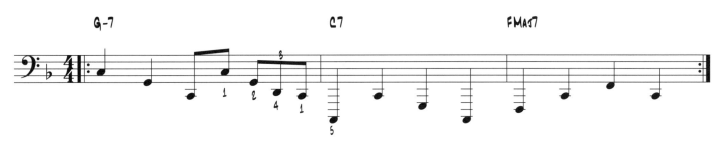

TUNES

Etude. "Consequences"

This tune is based on the chord changes to "It Could Happen to You," by Jimmy Van Heusen. It contains a *dominant pedal point* at the turnarounds (mm. 15–16, 30–32, and 47–48). Turnarounds are very conventional places in standard AABA tunes for pedal points.

The pedals in this tune are displaced rhythmically by adding a fifth to the octave. Notice how the right hand stretches the tonality at the pedal point areas (mm. 30–32 and 47–48). When the pedal is prolonged like this, there is a sense of outward modal shift to the overall tonality–a pull outside the tonality or the current key. (Stretching the tonality and "out playing" are discussed in chapter 19.)

Most of the embellishing motives used here are returning-note motives. These are quite accessible technically, and provide a strong forward pull to the left hand's rhythmic motion.

CONSEQUENCES

NEIL OLMSTEAD

Etude. "Evan's Up"

"Evan's Up," based on the chord changes to "All of You" by Cole Porter, begins with an introduction containing a tonic pedal point on E-flat. In measure 9, the tonic pedal moves to a dominant pedal point, finally (m. 16) resolving by step to inversions and roots of the given chords. The tonic pedal in measure 25 resolves in measure 32. This form repeats with a dominant pedal in measure 41 and another tonic pedal in measure 57.

The piece illustrates a multivoice contrapuntal texture, wherein active voices play off each other. The predominantly half-note bass rhythm lends itself more readily to *multivoice improvisation* (see chapters 14–16).

Unlike "Consequences," where pedal points were used at the turnarounds, "Evan's Up" uses them at the beginning of the A and B sections. This is consistent with conventional jazz interpretations of the piece "All of You."

Evan's Up

Neil Olmstead

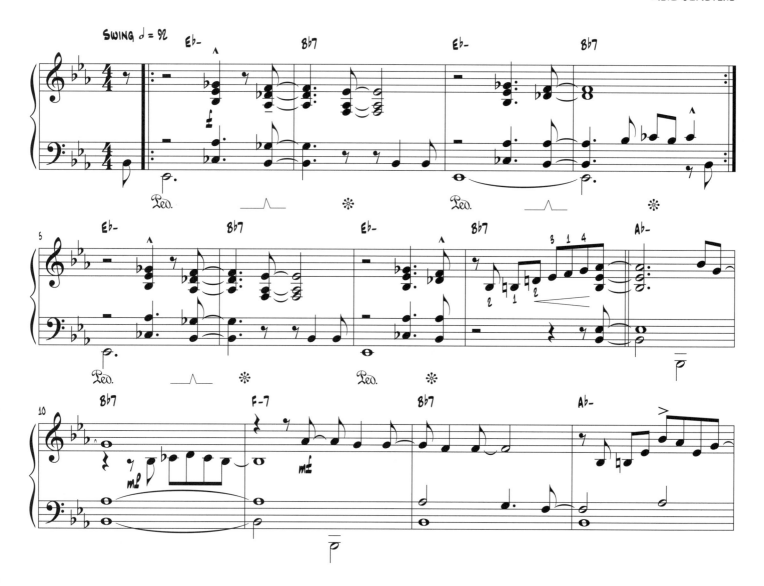

Lead Sheet. "Evan's Up"

In the lead sheet of "Evan's Up," apply pedal point in areas of the tune similar to the etude. These are the first eight measures of A and the first six measures of B. Explore your own ideas of pedal point as well. Use the CD for reference.

Lead Sheet. "Take A Breath"

"I'll Take Romance" by Oscar Hammerstein was the inspiration behind this tune. Try using pedal point in measures 13–16, or the beginning of the bridge. The last four measures would also be appropriate.

Take A Breath

Neil Olmstead

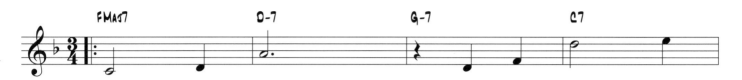

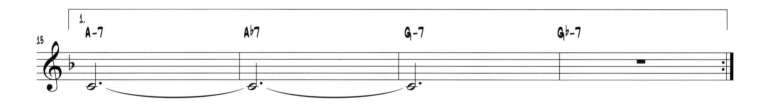

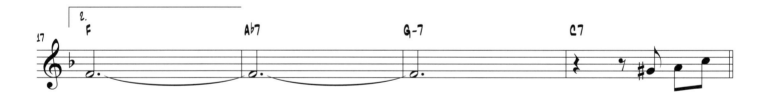

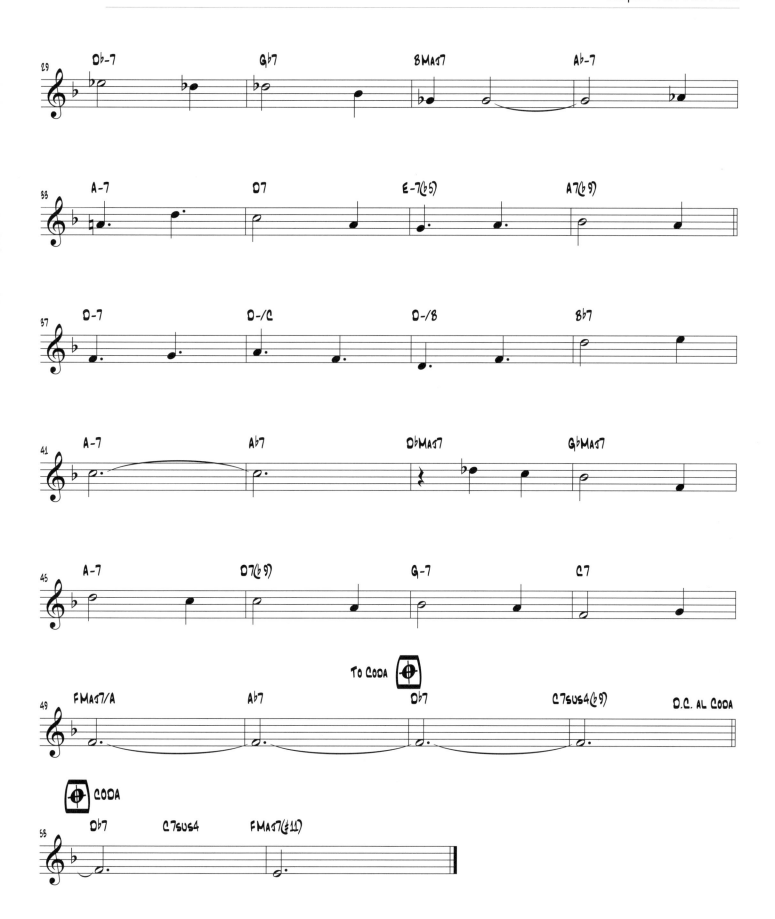

Chapter 11. The Blues and Beyond
Bass Motives for Blues Changes and Two-Fives

THEORY

Blues Motive

The *blues motive* is an essential characteristic of the blues bass line. This motive leaps from the chord's root either down a sixth or up to its third, and then continues in stepwise/chromatic motion. This helps to outline the bass line's harmony. It is called the "blues motive" because of its frequent use in the blues. This motive works best on dominant 7 chords and other major triad chords, but is generally avoided on minor chords.

- **Down a Sixth.** Leap down a sixth to the chord's major third. Then continue upwards chromatically to the next chord tone.

- **Up a Third.** Leap up a third to the chord's major third. Then continue upwards chromatically to the next chord tone.

Tip

Include a variety of motive types in your bass lines. These motives can sound patternistic, if used repeatedly, so it is always best to mix things up.

Alternate Motives for Two-Fives

In addition to the root-five motive (discussed previously), there are three *alternate motives* you can play for two-five progressions.

- **Alternate 1: Root-2-7-Root.** The first alternate motive for two-fives can be used on progressions set over four beats. It moves through the two-five in a simple ascending diatonic line of scale degrees 1-2-3-4. This places the seventh of the V chord on beat 3 (below, the note E-flat on the F7 chord and the note C on the D7[♭9]). This motive helps create smoother bass lines when the tempo is fast.

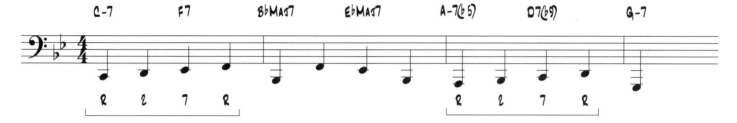

- **Alternate 2: R-2-3-R.** In the R-2-3-R motive, the root repeats at beat 4. This motive works well with two-fives set over eight beats.

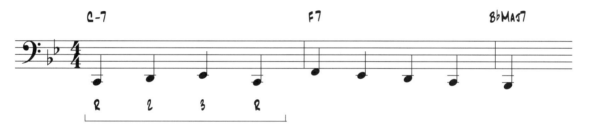

- **Alternate 3: R-2-3-5.** The third alternative motive, R-2-3-5, sets the fifth on beat 4.

Abbreviated Pedal

In the *abbreviated pedal,* the root is sustained above or below a root-five motive. This helps to fill out the harmony and adds a legato effect to the bass line. It is especially useful with medium-tempo tunes.

PRACTICE

Practice these exercises until you can play them fluently. Then try your own bass line and voicings. Mark all blues motives with a bracket (as shown in the first measure of exercise 1).

Comping Practice

Exercise 1. Blues Motive Practice

Exercise 2. Blues Motive Practice. Continue this bass line, and create your own right-hand voicings.

Exercise 3. Rhythm Changes. Play the left hand as written. Syncopate the right-hand voicings freely. In which measures do you notice the alternate motives?

TUNES

Etude. "Blues Man Soup"

"Blues Man Soup" contains numerous examples of this motive, some of which include an eighth-note *embellishing motive* (see m. 1).

Measure 3 shows the *ascending* form of the blues motive, leaping up a third. Measure 14 shows the *descending* form, leaping down a sixth, and then ascending in stepwise motion. Measure 15 is again an ascending form of the motive, with *embellishing motives* thrown in. Try analyzing the other left-hand material in this study.

BLUES MAN SOUP

Neil Olmstead

Lead Sheet. "Blues Man Soup"

Arrange "Blues Man Soup" using the blues motive discussed in this chapter. Use the CD for reference.

BLUES MAN SOUP

NEIL OLMSTEAD

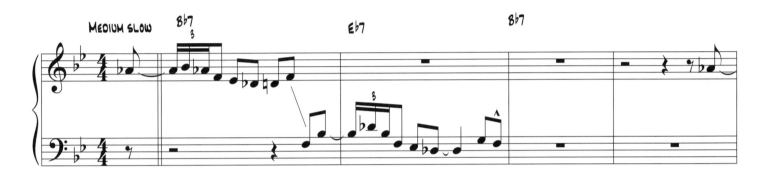

Lead Sheet. "Bop Stop"

This piece is based on the chord changes of Gershwin's "I Got Rhythm," probably the most famous jazz standard of all time. Try the alternate two-five motives in the A sections. Use the blues motive on the dominant chords in the bridge.

Chapter 12. Triads

Triadic Bass Lines and the Challenge of Stepwise Harmony

THEORY

Triads can add a great deal of harmonic color to a bass line—especially with changing chord functions over the same root (e.g., CMaj7 to C–7).

The standard "You and the Night and the Music" is a prime example of this. Its first phrase ends on C major, and its second phrase starts on C minor. Having the bass line outline these triads helps reinforce this relatively subtle change in harmony. "Alone Together" is another example. Here, the A section ends in D major, and it then repeats to the parallel minor chord at the top (DMaj7 to D–7). Again, triads in the bass line can bring out this harmonic shift.

So, when the chord function changes over the same root, triads in the bass line become useful, and often essential. Triads can be played in several different ways.

The Major Triad

As you saw in the previous chapter, the blues motive contains a downward leap of a sixth to the third of a major triad.

You can develop the blues motive into a complete triad. On beat 3, play the triad's fifth, leaping up a minor third. Then on beat 4, play a chord tone or a chromatic approach to the next root.

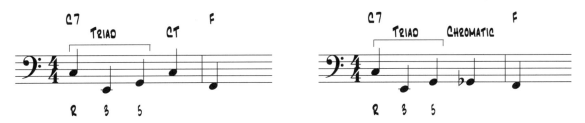

The Minor Triad

For minor triads, leap up to the third, and then descend back to the root on beat 3. Again, on beat 4, play a chord tone (such as the fifth) or a chromatic approach to the next root.

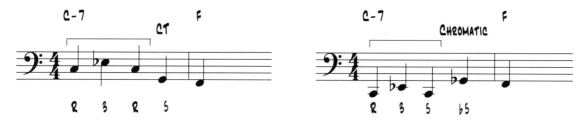

Note that all of these motives avoid the direct ascending or descending arpeggiated triad. Although bassists use them regularly, on the piano, they can easily sound overly simplistic and may detract from the bass line's linear momentum.

Avoid

However, Dave McKenna successfully uses ascending triads that are preceded by a chromatic approach. This dissonance breaks up what might otherwise seem like a formulaic recurring pattern.

Jazz Waltz

In 3/4 meter, slight variations on the above motives may be used. With only three beats, since the triad has three notes, there is no need for the chromatic approach or last chord tone on what was beat 4. Again, avoid the direct ascending or descending arpeggio.

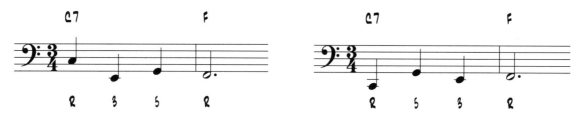

Stepwise Harmony

Another use for triadic bass lines is when the harmony descends by a series of whole or half steps. Tunes such as "Remember" or "Night and Day" are good examples of this type of progression.

It is difficult to create smooth bass lines with a descending stepwise progression. Used with the root-five and descending stepwise motives, triads can smooth out the line while reinforcing the harmonies. For the best effect in descending chord progressions, use a combination of triads, repeated notes, root-fives, and descending stepwise motives.

(Note: When using the descending stepwise motive, the downbeat following the motive requires the new chord's fifth. This is fine, providing you then move to the root. See mm. 3–4 below.)

PRACTICE

Triad Study

Practice "Triad Study" while comping in the right hand, using the chords shown and your own rhythms. Notice the use of triads in the bass.

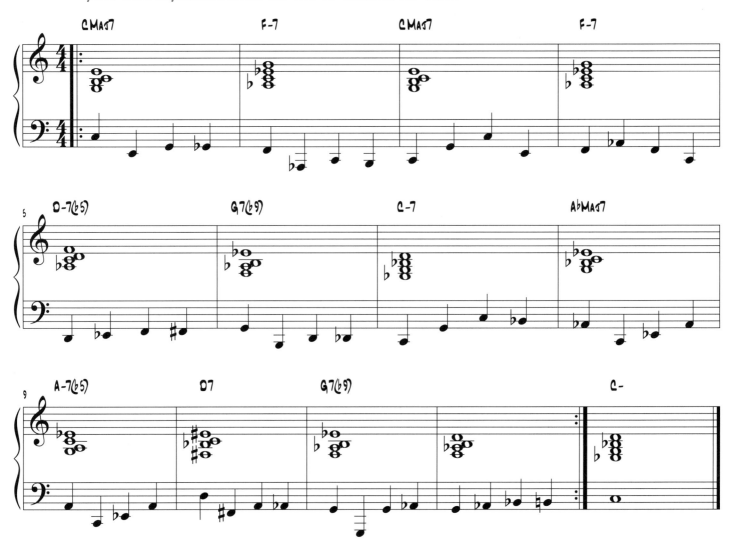

Stepwise Harmony Study

Practice the following progressions until you feel comfortable with the variety of motives used with descending stepwise harmony. Remember, when the chord progression descends by step, use a combination of stepwise, root-five, descending, and triadic motives.

Exercise 1. Stepwise Practice

Exercise 2. Stepwise Practice

TUNES

Etude. "Dave's Delight"

"Dave's Delight" is based on the chord changes to "Nobody Else But Me" by Jerome Kern. By focusing on triads, you'll find yourself playing many more thirds in the bass line. Sometimes, you'll play only the root and third (as in m. 18). Other times, you'll play the full triad (as in mm. 8, 10, and 11). At slow tempos such as this, triadic playing is very appropriate.

DAVE'S DELIGHT

NEIL OLMSTEAD

Lead Sheet. "Dave's Delight"

14

Practice "Dave's Delight" from the lead sheet, using it to create your own bass line and comping part. Try using many triads in your bass line.

Chapter 13. The Latin Connection
Root-Five Motives in Latin Grooves

THEORY

Latin Motives

The primary motives in a Latin bass line are drawn from the half-note motives, discussed in chapter 1. Root-five motives and root-octave motives are predominantly used in a straight-eighth-note rhythm.

Many Latin rhythms are used in jazz today, such as mambo, songo, samba, and cha cha cha. Our primary focus will be on a generic Latin rhythm based on the *bossa nova* beat.

One of the most common Latin bass motives is this one:

This motive can be made more pianistic by using an octave transposition of the root, instead of repeating it.

You can also use the octave based on the chord's fifth.

In cycle-five root motion, alternating octaves between the root and fifth creates smoother voice leading. It is also easier to play this motive, as your hand does not need to leap from root to root. Note that in measures 1–2 your hand remains over the C octave for two measures. The first C is the root and then becomes the fifth of F7. This alternating pattern continues.

Here is another bass pattern to explore:

PRACTICE

Latin Motives

Practice these exercises until you are comfortable with the bass patterns. Use the given voicings, and then create your own.

Exercise 1. Root-Fives

Practice the root-five motive over this Latin-feel progression.

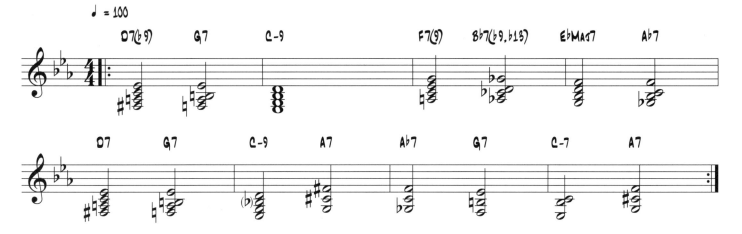

Exercise 2. Alternating Octaves

Practice alternating octaves between the root and fifth in this cycle-five progression. Try these comping rhythms.

THEORY

Balancing Activity Between Voices

Balancing activity between the hands will allow you more freedom of expression. It is not necessary to lock the left hand into a pattern. When the right hand is active, the left hand can ease back and just play half notes, ties, or even rest momentarily. The distinctive Latin rhythm will be carried by the right hand line, so there is no need to overstate it with left hand activity. Between right-hand phrases, the left hand can resume its active role, as shown below.

PRACTICE

Balancing Practice

Practice this samba melody with a bass line that balances the activity between the hands. For instance, at the end of each phrase, the left hand should become more active.

TUNES

Etude. "Double Time"

Practice "Double Time" until you are comfortable with this Latin groove. Notice that the bass line is fairly active during the comping passages, but becomes much simpler when the right hand improvises.

DOUBLE TIME

NEIL OLMSTEAD

Lead Sheet. "Dark Roast"

15

This lead sheet is based on the chord changes to Jobim's "O Grande Amour." Apply variations of the root-five motives for the head and solo. When soloing, balance the activity between your hands by simplifying the left hand for the more active right-hand passages.

DARK ROAST

NEIL OLMSTEAD

PART III. Multiple Voice Improvisation

Multiple voice improvisation means improvising several lines simultaneously. This requires a thorough linear understanding of the tune's harmony and organizing its chords' different voices to support their linear independence. The techniques in the next three chapters will help you gain confidence and fluidity with this style of improvising.

Your initial goal should be to gain melodic control over three simultaneous voices. A fourth voice may then be added as an accompanying voice. Organizing the voices in the traditional soprano, alto, tenor, bass format keeps things simple and clear. These are some general guidelines that will help you create linear independence in your voices.

1. **Range.** Keep each voice in its appropriate range. For piano purposes, the soprano and bass ranges can be extended, while the alto and tenor stay pretty much within the vocal ranges. Ranges can overlap to some degree.

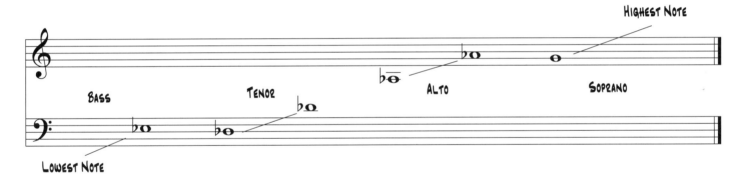

2. **Melodic Motion.** Think of the voices as a lead line (often soprano), bass line, and accompanying lines. Accompanying lines should stay within their ranges and move primarily by step. They will often have longer note values and more rests than the lead. The lead and bass have more freedom of movement, and will generally be more rhythmically active.

3. **Technique.** When working with three voices, the right hand generally takes the upper two voices. If a fourth voice is present, the tenor should be in the left hand with the bass. Hence, you will have two voices per hand.

4. **Repertoire.** Tunes with few melodic leaps work best for multiple-voice improvisation. These enable you to maintain control and develop the inner voices more easily. Some tunes that work well include "I Fall in Love Too Easily," "Everything I Love," "Blame It on My Youth," "Nobody Else But Me," "Old Folks," "Too Young to Go Steady," "Moon and Sand," "Why Should I Care," "The Old Country," "The Masquerade Is Over," and "Midnight Mood."

Chapter 14. Guide-Tone Lines

THEORY

In this chapter, we will discuss creating guide-tone lines, which are key to developing simultaneous linear voices. When you read a lead sheet, first work out the guide-tone lines of the progression.

Together with the chord root, *guide tones* are the essential components of a chord: the third and the seventh. *Guide-tone lines* are built from these essential notes. These lines have a strong sense of linear motion and independence. Using them as the basis for your accompaniment voices helps support a multivoice texture.

Move between guide tones by common tone or by step. When chords move within the circle of fifths, the guide-tone lines voice lead smoothly (by common tone or step) to notes of the opposite function, usually alternating between thirds and sevenths.

Below, the upper guide-tone line moves from the seventh of C–7 to the third of F7 to the seventh of B♭Maj7. The lower guide-tone line moves from the third of C–7 to the seventh of F7 to the third of B♭Maj7. Shifting positions on the same chord by inverting the guide tones is common. See G–7 below.

Play this circle-of-fifths progression, noting how the guide tones of each chord function.

Rule for Voice Leading

Voice-lead guide-tone lines primarily by step or common tone. Use mostly thirds and sevenths.

PRACTICE

Guide-Tone Practice

Starting with the voicing provided, play these progressions, with two guide-tone lines in the right hand and the given bass line in the left hand. If you voice-lead correctly and follow the cue chords, you will end with the last voicing given.

Exercise 1. Guide Tones

Exercise 2. Guide Tones

Exercise 3. Guide Tones

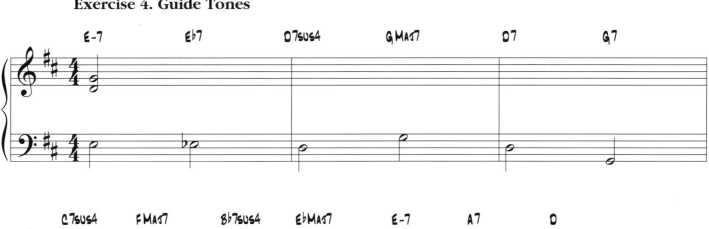

Exercise 4. Guide Tones

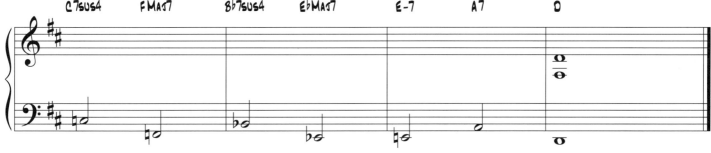

Using Guide Tones in Lead Sheets

> **Tip**
>
> When reading a lead sheet, first work out the guide-tone lines of the progression.

For the next three exercises, you will use this lead sheet.

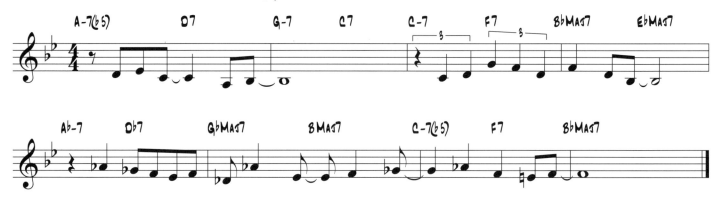

Exercise 1. Lead Sheet Practice

Work out the guide-tone lines using the cue notes provided.

Exercise 2. Lead Sheet Practice

Add a guide-tone line to the melody with your right hand.

Exercise 3. Lead Sheet Practice

Add a guide-tone line to the melody with your left hand.

Exercise 4. Lead Sheet Practice

Work out this melody with a guide-tone line and bass. Put a guide-tone line in your right hand. Then repeat this exercise with a guide-tone line in your left hand.

Exercise 5. Lead Sheet Practice

Work out this melody with a guide-tone line and bass. First, play the guide-tone line in your right hand, and then play it in your left hand.

Exercise 6. Lead Sheet Practice

Try exercises 4 and 5 again with two guide-tone lines and no bass. Note the implication of inversions. Inversions are commonly used to reharmonize tunes.

TUNES

Etude. "Old Coats"

"Old Coats" is based on the chord changes to the Willard Robison tune "Old Folks." Play the etude, and then do a thorough analysis of the inner voices. You will note that it begins with three voices: melody, bass, and alto. In measure 9, a fourth voice is added. Also note that some non-chord tones are used, for instance a passing tone in alto measure 9, and a suspension in alto measure 11. These are traditional uses of these non-chord tones; however, a more free approach can also be used. These will be discussed in a later chapter. Pay particular attention to the dynamic inflection of the individual voices.

OLD COATS

Neil Olmstead

Lead Sheet. "Old Coats"

16

Study the multivoice technique by starting with three voices, with the middle voice based on a guide-tone line. Then add a fourth voice, as discussed earlier.

OLD COATS

NEIL OLMSTEAD

Chapter 15. Non-Chord Tones

Passing Tones, Appoggiaturas, Suspensions, Neighbors, Pedal Points, and Inversions

THEORY

Non-chord tones are notes other than the chord's fundamental tones—the root, third, fifth, and seventh. These notes are named for their functions: suspensions, passing tones, neighbor notes, and others. Traditionally, there were many rules for how these notes could be used, but in jazz improvisation, there are fewer such limitations.

Non-chord tones can help you embellish the linear texture and simultaneously discover new harmonies that are created purely by melodic considerations. These are some of the non-chord tones you can use:

1. **Passing Tone.** A *passing tone* is a non-chord tone approached and left by step in the same direction. Below, the B-flat (measure 1, sixteenth before beat 3) is a passing tone, connecting chord tones A and C. The D on beat 4 is another passing tone, connecting the C and the E-flat.

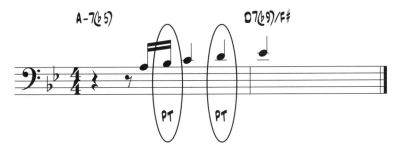

Here's how it looks in context:

2. **Appoggiatura.** An *appoggiatura* is approached by a leap and resolved by step in the opposite direction. Below, the alto's D on beat 4 is an appoggiatura, leaping up from the B-flat, and then resolving down by step to the C.

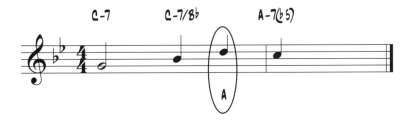

Here it is in context:

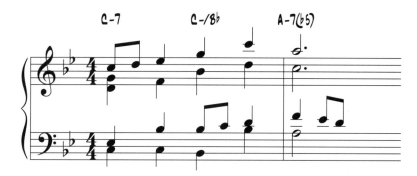

3. **Suspension.** A *suspension* is a chord tone or tension that is tied to the next chord, where it becomes a non-chord tone, and then resolves by step either down or up. The A on beat 3 is a fifth of D-7. It is suspended to the E-7(b5), and then resolves down to G.

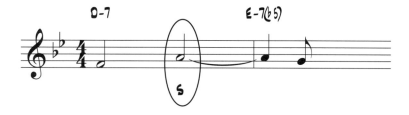

Here it is in context:

4. **Neighbors.** A *neighbor note* is a non-chord tone that is approached and left by step in opposite directions. The note A before beat 3 is a neighbor note to B-flat.

Here it is in context.

5. **Pedal Point.** A *pedal point* is a sustained (or repeated) tone, usually in the bass and usually the tonic or dominant of the key area. The bass note A is a dominant pedal point. We discussed pedal points in an earlier chapter.

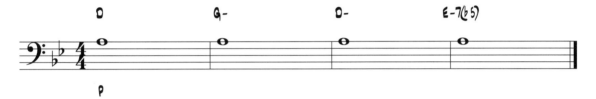

Here it is in context:

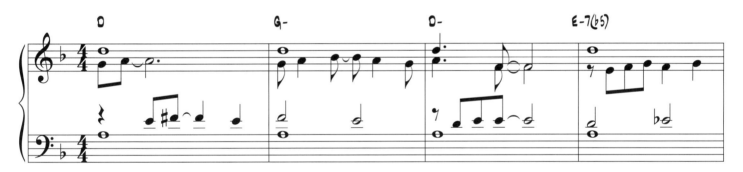

6. **Inversions.** Bringing the chord out of root position to first, second, or third inversion is a colorful reharmonization tool.

A Method for Adding Non-Chord Tones

When working with a lead sheet, follow this four-step process for enriching your harmonies.

1. Sketch the given harmony. The middle voices will move primarily by step; however, they may leap within a chord or at the start of a new phrase.

2. Add suspensions.

3. Add other non-chord tones.

4. Add inversions.

You will then have a complete four-part texture. This can be especially useful in your arrangement as an introduction, ending, or an interlude.

Let's try it with this lead sheet:

A method for discovering suspensions by ear at the piano

Play the four voices of the first chord.

1. Move the melody to the new chord, sustaining the lower voices.

2. Move the bass, sustaining the inner voices.

3. Restrike all tones—listen carefully for the suspension possibilities of the inner voices from the first chord to the second.

4. Move (resolve) the inner voices.

Choose an attractive suspension. Remember they can resolve upward or downward.

1. **Sketch the given harmony.** Create a harmonic sketch of the chords presented on the lead sheet. Sketch out chord voicings and guide-tone lines in a way that supports a multivoice texture.

2. Add suspensions. Explore the possibilities of suspensions by tying notes to the new harmonies. You may wish to simplify the rhythm of the melodic line so that the harmony will be heard more clearly. Resolve suspensions with diminuendo.

3. Add other non-chord tones. Finally, add passing tones, appoggiaturas, and neighbor notes as appropriate, indicated by ( ). Note frequent "re-struck" suspensions.

PRACTICE

Non-Chord Tones Practice

Apply the four-step approach to adding non-chord tones, using the following lead-sheet excerpts.

1. Sketch the given harmony.

2. Add suspensions.

3. Add other non-chord tones.

4. Add inversions.

> **Tip**
>
> Using these techniques may inspire a slowing of the tempo or a rubato feel. This enables better expression of the inflections and dynamics of the inner voices.

Exercise 1. Non-Chord Tones

Exercise 2. Non-Chord Tones

Exercise 3. Non-Chord Tones

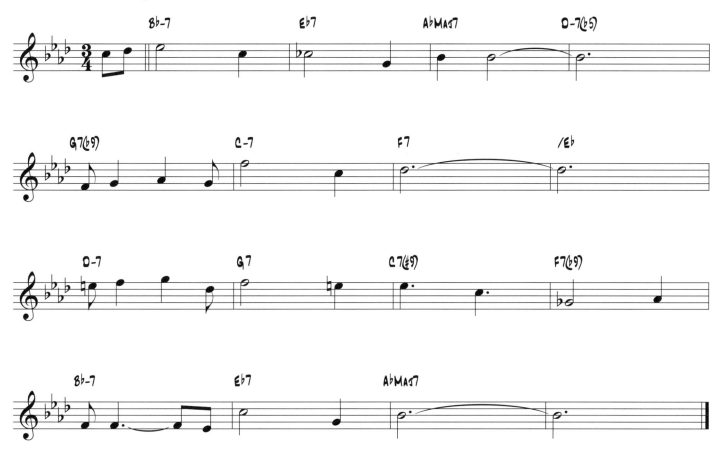

Exercise 4. Inversions. A fourth step includes placing inversions in the bass. This is an example of exercise 3 with inversions. Practice it a few times. Then try adding your own inversions.

TUNES

Etude. "Laura Lightly"

"Laura Lightly" is based on "Softly as in a Morning Sunrise" by Sigmund Romberg. This piece has a closely knit four-part texture. It illustrates how linking inner voices by step can create interesting voicings. The harmonies change frequently—every half measure or whole measure—which underscores the importance of using stepwise motion in these inner voices. Analyze the motion between these harmonies.

The piece begins with a pedal point in the outer voices. Note how the pedal point in the bass (mm. 1–4) gives way to inversions of chords (mm. 5–8). Long tones in some voices are contrasted with activity in others. All voices are rarely active simultaneously.

In this moderate-tempo Latin groove, try to sustain the long notes predominantly with your fingers, using the pedal only when necessary. This will help you develop the technique necessary to improvise in this texture.

LAURA LIGHTLY

NEIL OLMSTEAD

Lead Sheet. "Laura Lightly"

Practice lead sheet of "Laura Lightly" using the four-step approach.

1. Sketch the given harmony.

2. Add suspensions.

3. Add other non-chord tones.

4. Add inversions.

Chapter 16. The Melody in the Middle
Gaining Control of Three Voices

THEORY

In this chapter, we will learn an approach for developing multivoice arrangements where the melody is in voices other than the soprano.

1. **Study the melody.** Practice the melody, and observe its range. Consider which is the most effective voice for it: soprano, alto, or tenor.

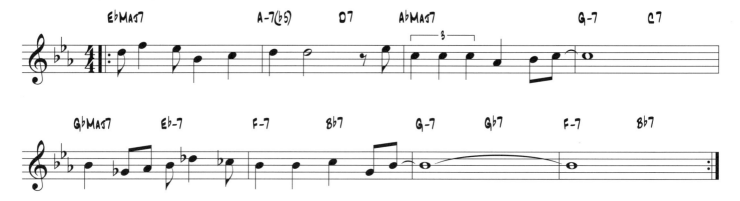

2. **Play the melody in the alto.** Using a rubato feel, practice the melody in the alto for a chorus, with the soprano harmonizing above it and the tenor resting. The bass should move by half notes. The soprano should move primarily by step, playing many long notes so that it sounds like an accompaniment to the alto.

3. **Harmonize the alto with the tenor.** Practice a chorus with the melody again in the alto, but this time, with the tenor playing the accompaniment. The soprano rests.

4. **Trade voices.** In the next chorus, trade melodic phrases between the soprano and the alto (melody shown in brackets, below). When one voice plays the melody, the other voice harmonizes. The tenor rests.

5. **Play four voices.** When you are comfortable playing three voices, add the tenor as the fourth voice. Keep the melody in the alto, with accompaniments in the soprano and tenor.

Now, you're ready to create your own arrangement. Consider the possibilities that this approach has revealed, and create your own arrangement of the melody based on which techniques you like best.

PRACTICE

Multivoice Improvisation

Practice the following exercises until you are comfortable playing multiple voices.

Exercise 1. Rock Ballad

1. Study and then play this rock ballad melody.

2. Play the melody in the tenor voice (left hand), transposed down an octave, along with the bass notes. Your right hand should rest. Practicing melodies in your left hand will help you develop flexibility in this technique.

3. Play the melody in the alto voice (right hand) with an active tenor voice and a bass line in the left hand.

4. Harmonize the alto melody with the soprano, above. Maintain an active tenor and bass. Hint: The tenor will follow the guide-tone line.

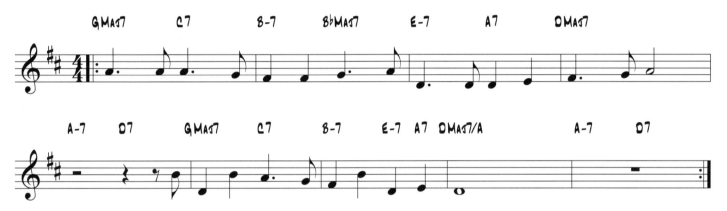

Exercise 2. Latin Melody

1. Study and then play this Latin melody.

2. Play the melody in the tenor voice (left hand). Add a bass accompaniment (left hand). Your right hand should rest.

3. Play the melody in the alto voice (right hand), harmonized by the soprano. Play an active bass line in your left hand.

4. Play the melody in the tenor voice (right hand) with an active alto accompaniment and bass line.

5. Try some inversions in the bass line.

Exercise 3. Jazz Waltz

1. Study and then play this jazz waltz melody.

2. Play the melody in the alto voice (right hand), harmonized by the soprano. Your left hand should play bass.

3. Starting with the melody in the alto, trade it freely back and forth between alto and soprano, one octave apart.

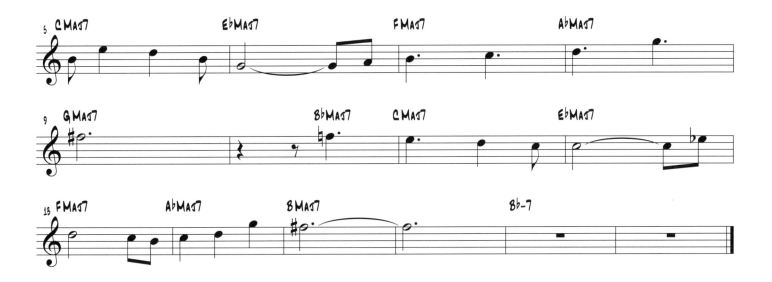

Exercise 4. Ballad

1. Study and then play this ballad.

2. Play both the bass and the melody (**8vb**) in the left hand.

3. Play this again adding a soprano obligato line in the right hand. The obligato line should begin on the last note of each phrase of the melody, as in the diagram below.

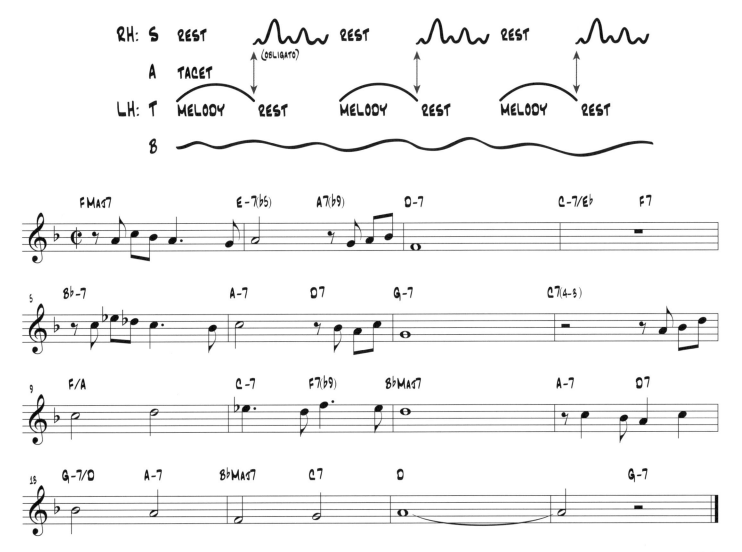

TUNES

Etude. "DAO"

"DAO" is based on the chord changes to the Benny Golson tune, "Whisper Not." It is illustrated here in a four-voice texture. The internal voices move in primarily stepwise motion, particularly between chord changes. This lends a cohesiveness to the individual voices, binding them together aurally and strengthening the harmonic fabric of the linear texture. Inversions in the bass line also help create a more varied harmonic texture.

Note the imitative qualities between voices, such as alto measure 15 and tenor measure 16; and tenor measure 29 and soprano measure 30.

When you practice improvising in this multivoice texture, a rubato time feel is the most accessible and easiest approach. Clear expressive dynamic color is necessary, and it is best approached with open time, unrestrained by meter limitations.

DAO

Neil Olmstead

Lead Sheet. "DAO"

18

Practice "DAO" from the lead sheet. Use the approach suggested in this chapter.

Critical Tools

Practice this approach on all tunes.

1. Study the melody.

2. In the LH alone, play the bass and melody in the tenor.

3. Play the melody in the alto and the harmony in the soprano.

4. Play the melody in the alto, harmonized with the tenor.

5. Trade the melody between the alto and tenor.

6. Add a fourth voice.

DAO

Neil Olmstead

Chapter 17. Rhythmic Freedom
Ties and Concerted Rhythms

THEORY

The many possibilities inherent in rhythmic development can open up your music and broaden the freedom of your playing. Earlier, we introduced rhythmic variety in the left hand by mixing half-note and quarter-note motives. Additionally, dots, ties, and concerted rhythms can all help to enhance the independence of the bass and add rhythmic vitality to the piece.

Ties help prolong the resolution to a new chord's root. By tying bass notes over the barline and delaying the new root, a higher level of abstraction is introduced to the harmony, rhythm, and form of the music.

Below, in measure 1, the bass note A on beat 4 is tied into the next measure. This A is the fifth of the D minor chord. It is prolonged into the next measure, where it moves to the fifth of A7(♭9). This introduces an interesting rhythmic interplay between the roots and fifths of the chords that follow; the root of D minor in measure 3 is not stated until beat 4.

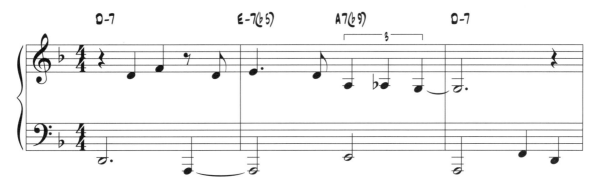

This level of ambiguity is typical of rhythmically free playing. Because the form is retained, there is a natural pull towards the chordal roots and tonal centers of the piece. This pull heightens the tension-resolution element of the tonal improvisation that is occurring. Such enhancements of the rhythmically dramatic elements are vital for developing creative and free playing.

PRACTICE

Rhythmic Freedom Practice

Exercise 1. Tie Practice. Practice this exercise, and notice how the ties help delay the resolutions.

Exercise 2. Comping Practice. Practice this progression, using ties freely while comping in the right hand.

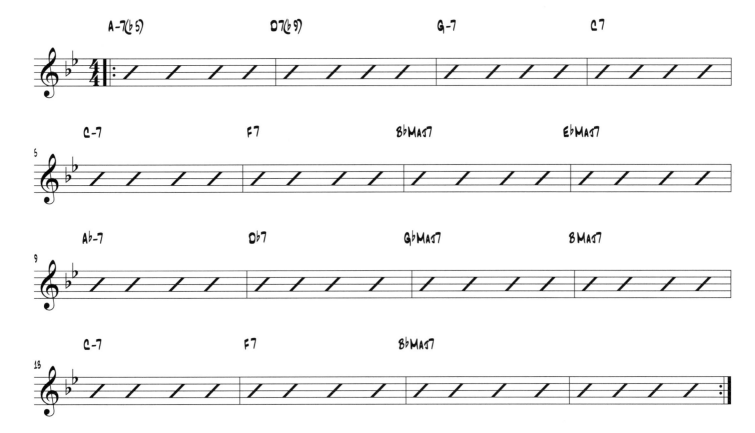

THEORY

Concerted Rhythms

A *concerted rhythm* is when both hands play the same rhythms simultaneously, but not necessarily the same notes.

Concerted rhythms enhance the rhythmic freedom of the bass and further energize the right hand's improvisation. It is often relatively easy for the left hand to imitate the right hand's rhythm, and this can give the music a powerful accent. In the example below, the left hand is in free melodic counterpoint to the right hand, but uses the identical rhythm. (Also, see "Singularity," later this chapter, m. 5 and mm. 43–44).

Your hands can also be concerted both rhythmically and melodically. This requires a bit more technique, but it results in a rhythmically driving melodic line. (Also, see "Singularity" mm. 30–32.)

PRACTICE

Concerted Rhythms Practice

Exercise 1. Concerted Rhythms. Play the first sixteen measures as written. Then play the next sixteen-measure right-hand line while improvising a bass line that includes some concerted rhythms.

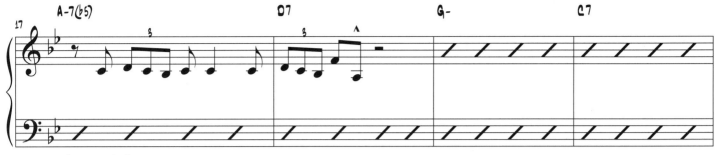

Continue L.H., add concerted rhythms

Exercise 2. Concerted Rhythms. Practice this exercise as written.

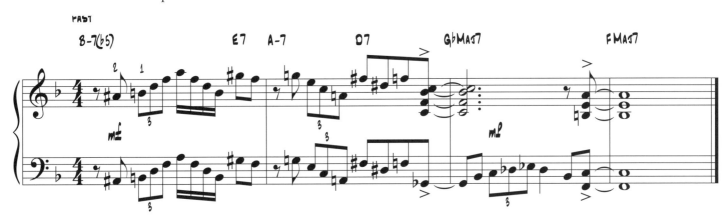

Exercise 3. Concerted Rhythms. Practice this exercise as written. This short ending is an example of how a concerted line can be used to end a tune.

TUNES

Etude. "Singularity"

This piece is based on the chord changes to Dietz and Schwartz's tune "Alone Together." The chord changes may appear to be inconsistent with the bass line. However, this study represents the use of tied notes and other elements of rhythmic freedom. This lends an abstraction to the harmony and enhances the rhythm of the left-hand line. The original chord changes are written so that you may analyze the bass in relation to those non-chord tones.

To balance the rhythmic activity of both voices, it may be helpful to trade activity in both hands. Play long tones in the left hand while improvising in the right hand. Then rest in the right hand while playing more actively in the left hand. Notice measures 6 to 8. Where else does this occur? And how would you analyze the rhythm of measures 21 to 22?

SINGULARITY

Neil Olmstead

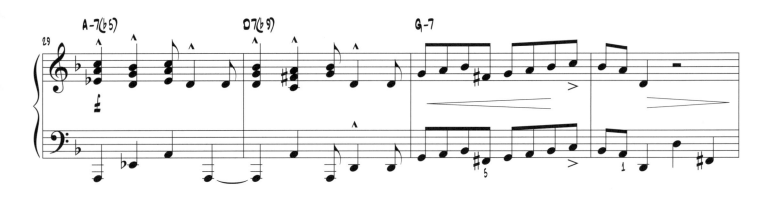

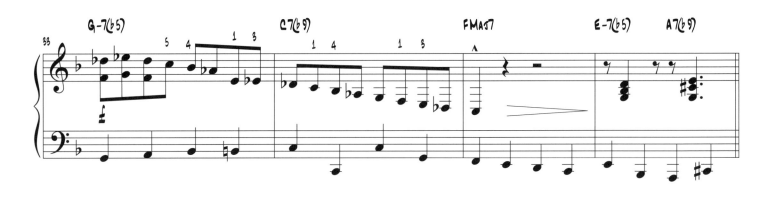

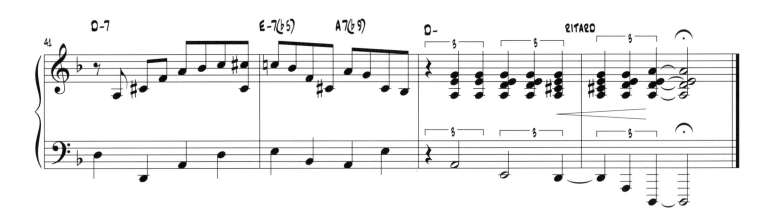

Lead Sheet. "Singularity"

Use the lead sheet to create your own arrangement of "Singularity." Use ties and concerted rhythms.

Chapter 18. Melodic Freedom
Free Melody, and Appogiaturas and Passing Tones

THEORY

In a bass line, bass motives can be interspersed with free melodic ideas. While the left hand departs from the motives, the right hand rests or comps. The left-hand line may rise out of the bass register and play melodically, as if it were soloing. Then, it returns to the functional bass motives, and the right hand resumes its usual role, improvising or playing melody.

In measures 3–4, below, the bass plays melodically while the right hand rests. (Also, see "Jester Play" later in this chapter, mm. 7–8 and 11–12.)

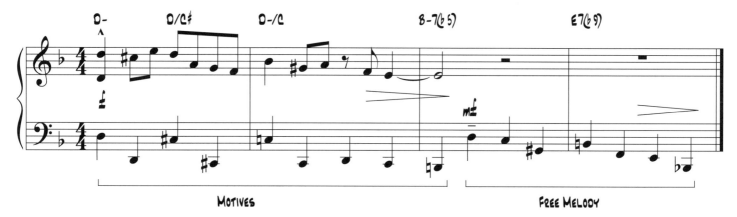

Follow these guidelines for incorporating melody into your bass line:

1. Leave enough space around the free line to open and resolve it.

2. Pace the individual phrases in a manner similar to "trading," as if two voices were conversing. When you trade, instruments (or voices) alternate playing solo phrases.

3. The right-hand line can overlap the left-hand line, particularly near the end of the phrases (e.g., the right hand comes in before the left-hand's melody has resolved). This creates an "elision" of the two voices. This area can be a point of departure for other "free" playing, so try expanding it.

Non-Chord Tones on the Strong Beat

Another way to add melodic freedom to your bass lines is by using non-chord tones. A line's shape generally takes precedence over its harmony. This means that you may play a non-chord tone on the downbeat of a measure. This works, as long as you then resolve to the chord root. These late resolutions are like "appoggiaturas" or "descending passing tones" in traditional counterpoint. They are both non-chord tones set on strong beats, which then resolve to chord tones.

- An *appoggiatura* is approached by leap and then resolved by step in the opposite direction.

- A *descending passing tone* is approached by step and then resolved by step in the same direction.

Both of these dissonances are common in traditional tonal music, and should be used freely in jazz improvisation as well. If you think you've blundered by not reaching the root "on time," fear not; you have probably just played a justifiable non-chord tone.

Free melody in bass should have a dynamic inflection that gives it prominence as a viable melody.

PRACTICE

Free Melody Practice

These exercises will help you practice incorporating free melody into your left-hand lines. Play them as written. Then repeat them while improvising your own free melody bass in the measures indicated.

Exercise 1. Free Melody

Exercise 2. Free Melody

Exercise 3. Free Melody

Exercise 4. Free Melody

Exercise 5. Free Melody

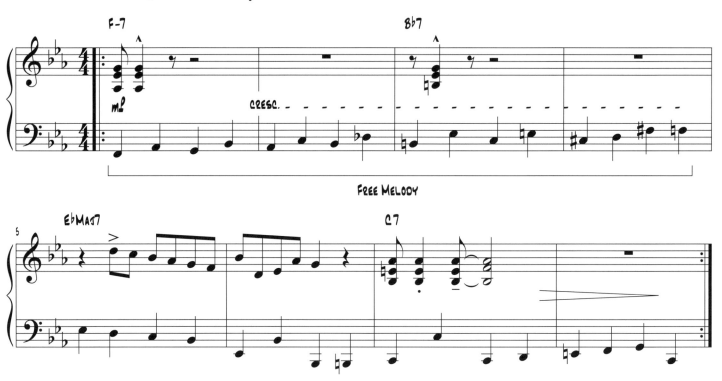

Exercise 6. Free Melody

Exercise 7. Free Melody. Create your own comping part. Analyze the bass line for motives and free melody.

Exercise 8. Free Melody. Practice a bass line against a simple comping part, placing some non-chord tones on the V7 chords.

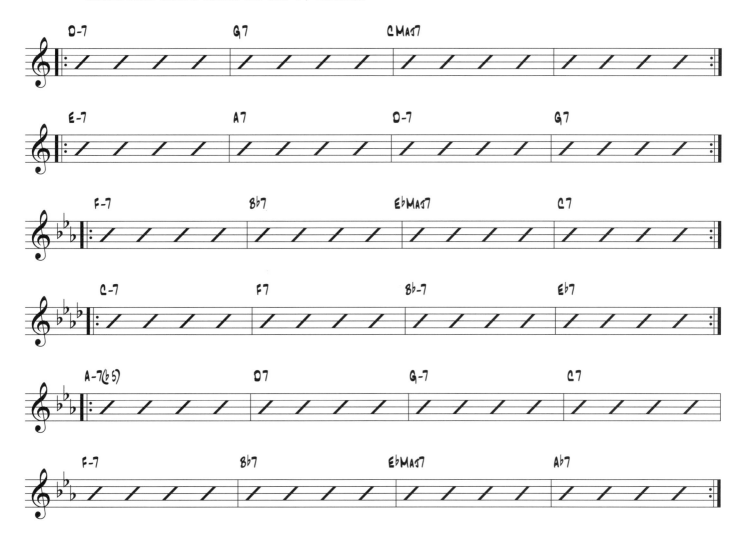

Exercise 9. Free Melody. Practice a bass line against a simple comping part, placing some non-chord tones on the V7 chords and the minor 7 chords.

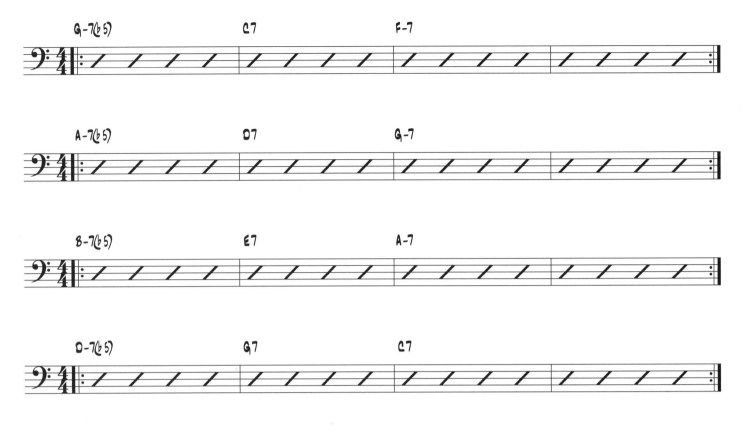

Exercise 10. Free Melody. Next, place the non-chord tones on the dominant 7 and IMaj7 chords.

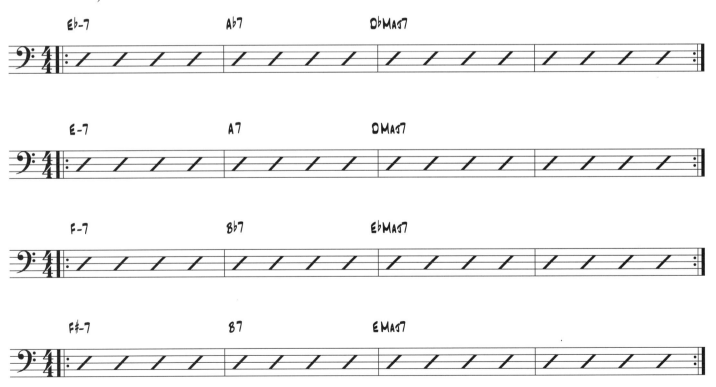

TUNES

Etude. "Jester Play"

This piece is based on the chord changes to Jerome Kern's "Yesterdays." Note how the left hand rises out of the bass register (often leaping), and plays melodically, while the right hand rests or comps. The left hand then resumes a functional bass, playing motives to accompany the right hand improvisation.

Jester Play

Neil Olmstead

Lead Sheet. "Jester Play"

20

This lead sheet is also based on the chord changes to "Yesterdays," by Jerome Kern. Listen to the CD for reference. Then practice the tune using a variety of free melody ideas between your right hand's improvised phrases.

JESTER PLAY

Neil Olmstead

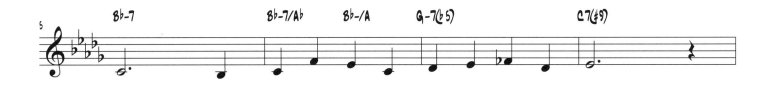

Chapter 19. Tristano Techniques
Embellished Pedal Points and Modes

The original recording of Lennie Tristano's LP *The New Tristano* (1962) includes some of the most interesting examples of free contrapuntal jazz improvisation. Listen to two tracks in particular: "C Minor Complex" and "G Minor Complex."

In "C Minor Complex," Tristano sets up a mode at the beginning by combining scalar material with chordal sonorities. Though it sounds as if he's using a chord progression, he proceeds to improvise through a series of progressions and cadences in C minor that are tonally logical, but devoid of form. He continues with aggressive linear phrases in the right hand, often using pedal points in the left. Sometimes, he repeats a right-hand pattern extensively, which brings the left hand into focus, as it moves more freely. Thick chordal clusters repeat in displaced rhythms, and then revert back to Tristano's signature linear character, which brings the piece to a close, back in C minor. It lasts 7.5 minutes, and maintains an unrelenting driving character throughout.

Tristano's music reveals the possibilities that lie in the world of free modal improvisation. In this chapter, we will use two techniques that are much in evidence in these recordings: chromatically embellished pedal point, and the use of modes. Concerted rhythms, discussed earlier, are another element that Tristano uses extensively. All these techniques are effective on many jazz standards.

THEORY

Chromatically Embellished Pedal Point

We have seen how dominant or tonic pedal points can be sustained in the left hand, while the right hand improvisation continues through the tune's form. This pedal point can be chromatically embellished to add increased tension and abstraction to the texture. The improvisation against it can be developed motivically, or it may use the imitative techniques discussed in chapter 21. Pedal points may infer modal qualities, and may indeed lead to modal improvisation.

PRACTICE

Tristano-Style Free Improvisation

Exercise 1. Pedal Points

Practice this dominant pedal point first with the traditional pedal point and then with the chromatically enhanced pedal point. Then transpose it up half a step, playing it in the key of D-flat.

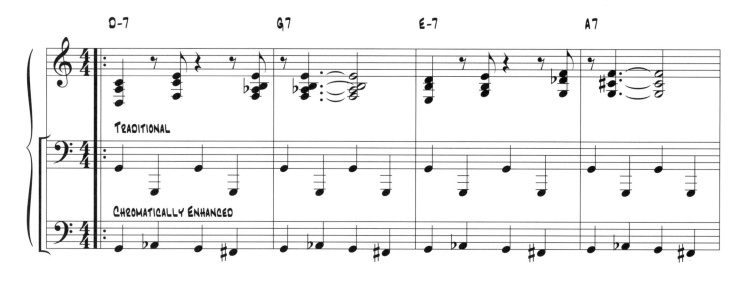

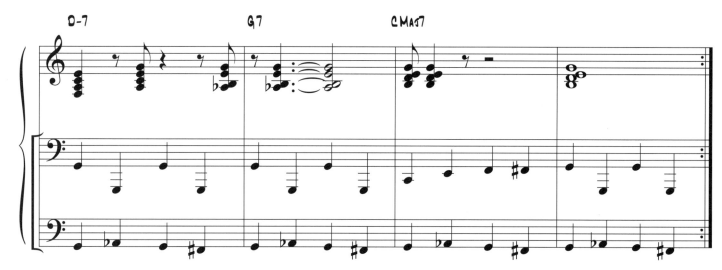

Exercise 2. Pedal Points. Practice both pedal points while comping in the right hand, using your own rhythms. Then try an improvisation against the enhanced pedal point.

Exercise 3. Pedal Points. Using this progression, explore pedal points that lead to modal improvisation. (See appendix C for a review of modes and jazz scales.)

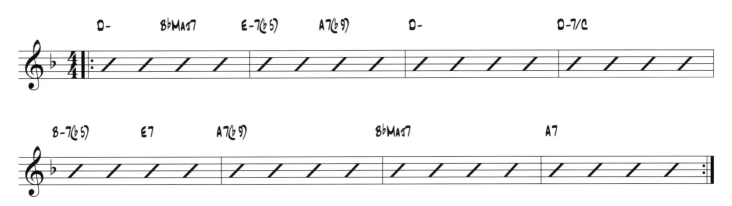

Exercise 4. Modal Tunes: "Dania." Many modal tunes shift abruptly from mode to mode. On the next two exercises, practice comping with a bass line on these progressions. Then improvise in the right hand, moving from mode to mode. In "Dania," the modes are labeled for you.

DANIA

Neil Olmstead

Exercise 5. Modal Tunes: "Marissa." Which modes would work here?

Marissa

Neil Olmstead

Exercise 6. Modal Regions: "Anna Be Modal." This next lead sheet will help you practice improvising by using a modal approach over entire tonal areas of a piece. If a tune's A section is in a minor key and its B section is in a major key, you can improvise in the minor mode for the whole A section, with only minimal reference to the actual chord progression. In the B section, you might return to a more traditional style of playing, based more on using chord tones.

After improvising traditionally on "Anna Be Modal," try a minor mode improvisation on the A section and a major mode improvisation on the B section.

ANNA BE MODAL

Neil Olmstead

TUNES

Etude. "Ultra Violet"

"Ultra Violet" is based on the chord changes to "Solar" by Miles Davis. The piece begins with motivic development in the right-hand solo over a traditional-motive bass line. The second chorus (m. 13) starts with a pedal point. This pedal point is reiterated in the third chorus, and it becomes the basis for a modal improvisation that expands outward from the harmonies of the tune. The piece ends in an entirely different mode, B-flat minor. Analyze "Ultra Violet" and then play it at a brisk tempo.

ULTRA VIOLET

Neil Olmstead

Lead Sheet. "Ultra Violet"

Practice "Ultra Violet." Try using a dominant pedal point to inspire a modal improvisation.

Chapter 20. Metric Modulation
Rhythmic and Metric Shifts

THEORY

A *metric modulation* is a shift in rhythmic groove, meter, or both.

Rhythmic Groove Modulation

In "Ballad to Swing" (chapter 4), when we shifted between cut-time ballad (2/2) and swing (4/4) grooves, we changed the groove by using different rhythms in the right hand, while the harmonic rhythm remained constant.

As we saw, using rhythms based on different subdivisions of the measure can shift the groove to a different feel. For example, to modulate from 2/2 to 4/4, speed up the rhythms so that they are more oriented to the quarter note rather than to the half note. Instead of straight eighth notes and quarter-note triplets, use swing eighths and eighth-note triplets.

This type of rhythmic shift changes the feel and groove, but not the actual meter. The basic meter remains at four quarter notes per measure, and the half-note line in the left hand continues throughout. The groove changes from a two-feel to a four-feel, but the actual quarter note and harmonic rhythm remain constant.

Metric Modulation

A second type of metric modulation is to change the meter, for example, shifting from 4/4 to 3/4 with the quarter note staying constant. These shifts usually occur at significant landmarks within the form, such as at the bridge or at the start of a new chorus.

Bill Evans loved metric modulation and used it in such tunes as "Comrade Conrad" and "How My Heart Sings." Denny Zietlan uses it on "All the Things You Are," where the bridge goes to 3/4 and then moves back to 4/4. The rhythmic groove stays constant but the meter changes. The harmonic rhythm expands, then contracts by one beat.

Rhythmic Groove and Meter Change

Changing both the groove and the meter is also common, and it requires more practice. In this type of modulation, the value of the pulse changes. For example, you may shift from 3/4 to 4/4. Instead of simply changing the emphasis of the quarter-note pulse, the pulse shifts to another note value, such as the dotted quarter. This lets you change the perceived tempo, as well as meter and groove. The actual tempo and harmonic rhythm remain the same, however. (Listen to Bill Evans' "Waltz for Debby" on the *Piano Player* CD for a trio version of this type of modulation.)

This excerpt from "Green Tea" begins in 3/4, and then modulates to a slower groove in 4/4. The modulation begins with a dotted-quarter-note pattern in the bass, which is then matched by the right-hand line. This becomes a two feel, which finally transitions into 4/4. The quarter note in the new groove continues at the same tempo as the dotted quarter note in the old one. The harmonic rhythm is constant.

To reverse this modulation, returning to 3/4, the right hand plays quarter-note triplets while the left hand plays half notes. The quarter-note triplets become quarter notes of 3/4. The left hand matches that quarter note. (See Practice Exercise 3.)

Critical Tools: Common Metric Modulations

Groove Changes

- Ballad (two feel) to swing (four feel): quarter note constant
- Swing to double-time feel: quarter note constant
- Ballad half-time feel to 12/8 (or 6/8) blues feel: quarter note constant

Meter Changes

- 4/4 to 3/4 with constant quarter note and groove
- 3/4 to 4/4 with constant quarter note and groove

Meter and Groove Changes

- 3/4 to 4/4 with:

- 4/4 to 3/4 with:

Putting medium tempo and up tempo 4/4 tunes in 3/4 without changing the harmonic rhythm presents a critical challenge. Follow these steps.

Practice the 4/4 tune in 3/4.

Formula:

1. Play half notes in the LH creating a cut-time feel.
2. Play a half-note triplet against that in the RH.
3. Match the half-note triplet rhythm in the LH.

This is the new 3/4 meter.

Further challenge:

1. Play the 4/4 tune with quarter notes in the left hand.
2. Play some quarter-note triplets in a duplet melodic shape in the RH.
3. Accent every other note of the triplets.
4. Tie every other note of the quarter-note triplets, creating half-note triplets.
5. Match the half-note triplet rhythm in the LH.

This is the new 3/4 meter.

PRACTICE

Metric Modulation Practice

Practice the following metric modulation exercises until you're comfortable with the shifting times and grooves. Using the material and terms of this chapter, how would you identify and describe each of these metric modulations?

Practice moving back and forth between 3/4 and 4/4 as frequently as you can. Try delaying the resolution to the new time feel by stretching out the transition between meter changes. At this moment, you are actually playing in two time feels simultaneously!

Exercise 1. Groove Change

Exercise 2. Meter Change

Exercise 3. Meter and Groove Change

Exercise 4. Ballad to 12/8 Feel

24

Exercise 5. Slowing the Tempo

Exercise 6. Slowing then Increasing the Tempo (3/4 to 2/4 to 3/4)

Exercise 7. Metric Modulation Progression. In the next three exercises, practice metrically modulating over each progression, repeating until you can play it easily. Improvise both a bass line and a comping part. For this progression, modulate from cut time to quarter time, then back to cut time.

Exercise 8. Metric Modulation Progression. Modulate from cut time to 6/8 blues, then back to cut time.

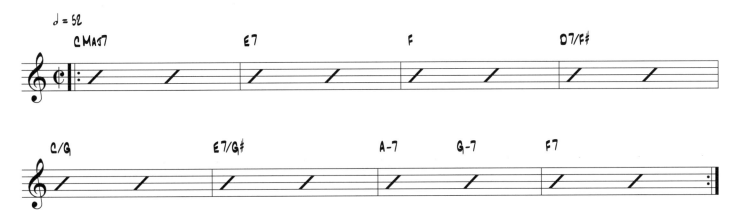

Exercise 9. Metric Modulation Progression. Modulate from 2/4 to 3/4 (♩ = ♩) to 4/4 (♩. = ♩).

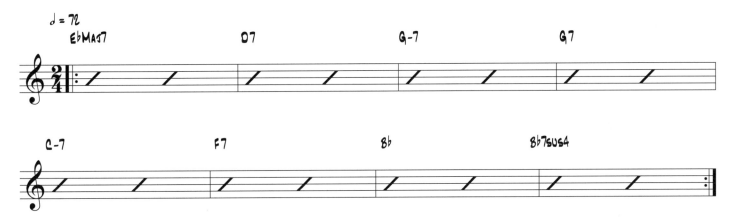

> **Hint**
>
> Try to lengthen the transition points so that you can feel two time-feels concurrently.

CHALLENGE

Using the progression to exercise 9, can you modulate as shown below?

Invent some metric modulations of your own.

TUNES

Etude. "All the Tongs"

This variation on "All the Things You Are," by Jerome Kern, demonstrates a metric modulation from 3/4 to 4/4 with the quarter note remaining constant. There is no change in the groove or tempo; the meter simply changes. After setting up the jazz waltz feel, the music modulates abruptly to 4/4 at the second ending. The groove and tempo remain constant as the meter changes. At measure 28, the tune moves back to 3/4 with a syncopated bass. However, the groove is basically the same. (Note the abbreviated pedal in mm. 29–37.) At measure 42, the piece moves back to 4/4 with the walking bass continuing uninterrupted.

ALL THE TONGS

NEIL OLMSTEAD

Etude: "Green Tea"

Based on the chord changes to the Churchill tune, "Some Day My Prince Will Come," this piece demonstrates the ease in which one may perform a metric modulation. This tune goes from 3/4 to 4/4 and back with the tempo and groove also changing.

In measures 35–39, the dotted quarter note of 3/4 becomes the quarter note pulse of 4/4. In simplifying the right hand improvisation by playing dotted quarter rhythms in both hands, the player then shifts to 4/4 with the new quarter note being equal to the old dotted quarter note. The time seems to slow down, but in fact, the harmonic rhythm goes from three beats to two beats within the same period of time.

When practicing this, stay with the dotted quarter note in the right hand line as long as necessary, until you are comfortably in a solid two-beat rhythm. Eventually, make the switch to 4/4, with a harmonic change every two beats.

Measures 52–55 illustrate the move from 3/4 to 4/4 by using the quarter-note triplet as the common denominator. The right-hand improvisation begins playing the triplet in measure 53 and the left hand matches it in measure 54. Then both hands play the quarter-note triplet rhythm as a quarter note of 3/4 in measure 55.

This process can be simplified by the left hand playing half notes in 4/4 while the right hand plays triplets.

GREEN TEA

NEIL OLMSTEAD

Lead Sheet. "Green Tea"

Practice "Green Tea" from the lead sheet, using it to create your own arrangement. Try moving to 4/4 by way of the quadruplet. Then return to 3/4 by using the quarter-note triplet. What other ways can you find to modulate?

Chapter 21. Motivic Development and Imitation
Imitation/Variation and Pitch Gradation

THEORY

Motivic Development

A Motive is a short melodic idea that when developed, by repetition and/or variation, gives logical coherence to a phrase group or solo. Indeed, motives often require development in order to complete an idea.

Repeating a short melodic phrase gives it a sense of completion. By remembering what we play long enough to restate it in some manner, we can achieve a horizontal sense in our music. Rather than just feeding off the chord of the moment, we can use our motivic ideas to inspire our next phrase. Then the listener will feel that what they are hearing is based on something that they remember. Some motivic improvisers include: Miles Davis, Thelonious Monk, Herbie Hancock, Keith Jarrett, and Enrico Piernunzi. Many melodies of standard tunes are composed motivically: "Whisper Not," "Dolphin Dance," "My Funny Valentine," "The Boy Next Door."

Framing a motive by rest gives it focus and an expectation of development. A motive is developed by imitating the shape, rhythm, duration, and articulation.

Analysis exercise: Analyze this phrase group. How many different motives do you see in these 16 measures? How are they developed? See the complete etude later in this chapter.

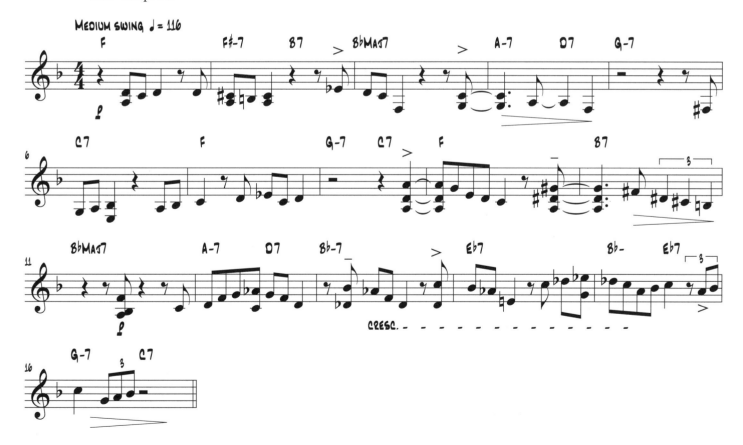

PRACTICE

> **Practice Tips for Motivic Development and Improvisation**
>
> 1. Choose tunes that you can play easily so that you can concentrate fully on improvisation. Some standards that work well for improvisation practice include "I Love You," "Tune Up," "Blue Monk," and "Beautiful Love."
>
> 2. Try using motives from the tune's melody.
>
> 3. When concentrating on right-hand lines, use simple left-hand accompaniments (half notes and whole notes).
>
> 4. Especially when you are beginning to practice improvisation, use short ideas or motives (three notes or so). These motives are brief enough so that you can recall them easy, and usually "require" that you develop them, in order to be complete.
>
> 5. Follow each phrase with a rest. This rest will be essential in helping you remember your improvised phrases.
>
> 6. Strive to justify every note by developing it or having it become part of a new idea that will be developed. Again, make your phrases short, and follow each phrase with a rest.
>
> 7. Repeat a shape as many times as you feel it has musical merit.

Exercise 1. Motivic Practice

On this blues progression, practice developing a solo by using imitation and variation. Focus on the practice tips listed above, and use the following approach.

- Improvise a short, concise shape (idea/motive). Then rest.

- Repeat that shape at the same pitch level. Then rest.

- Play a new shape. Then rest.

- Repeat the second shape at a different pitch level. Then rest.

- Repeat the second shape again at either the same or a different pitch level.

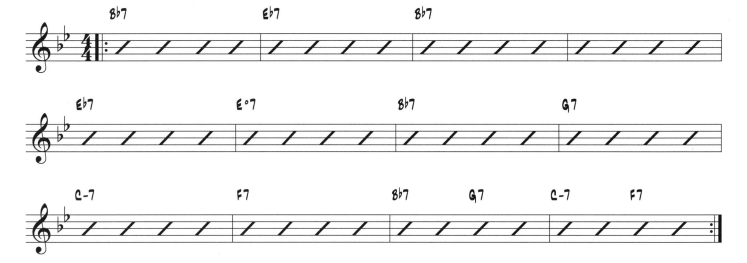

Here's an example of how your solo might turn out.

You could analyze the form of the above improvisation like this:

Though exact repetition of an idea can be effective, imitation that is too precise and predictable may lack a creative pulse. Varying the idea will help you avoid having it sound redundant or stale. For example, you may vary the pitches.

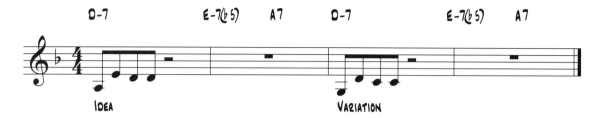

Playing the idea at the same pitch level but at a different point in time may increase tension towards completion. Here, the idea begins on beat 2, rather than beat 1.

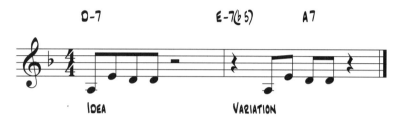

The above technique can be extended to complete the idea. By ending on a strong beat near the tonic chord, the original idea will sound more finalized and complete. Depending on the relationship of the phrase to the meter and harmony, this can be effective.

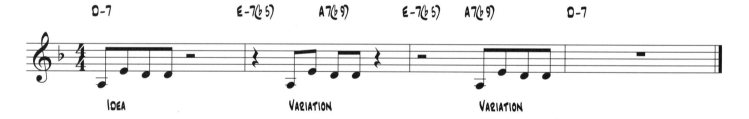

Rhythmic variation is another type of imitation. Here, the rhythms of the original idea are expanded.

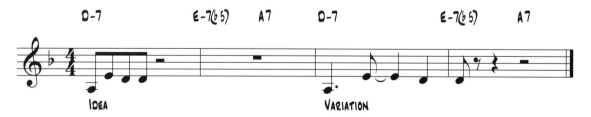

DEVELOPING THE MUSICAL CHARACTERISTICS

You can open up developmental possibilities by focusing on each essential musical characteristic of your motive—shape, duration, rhythm, dynamics, and articulation. Play with these essential characteristics of your motives by practicing both similar and opposite elements in your improvisations.

Musical Characteristics

The following list of musical characteristics should be practiced in the order below. Strive for 100 percent accuracy by repeating every idea with its musical character before creating a new idea. Play a complete chorus on each.

1. Shape

   - Descending. Play a phrase that moves from a higher to a lower pitch.
   - Ascending to Descending. Play a phrase that moves up and then down, forming an arch.
   - Ascending. Play a phrase that moves from a lower to a higher pitch.

2. Dynamics

   - Diminuendo. Play a phrase or motive that decreases in volume.
   - Crescendo to diminuendo. Play a phrase or motive that increases and then decreases in volume.
   - Crescendo. Play a phrase or motive that increases in volume.

Combine Dynamics with Shape

   - Play a descending phrase with a diminuendo.
   - Play a phrase that ascends with a crescendo and then descends with a diminuendo.

3. Inflections

   - Accent (>). Play the first note of a motive louder than the others.
   - Legato (–). Play all notes of your motive smoothly and connected.
   - Staccato (.). Play all notes of your motive short.

Combine inflections with dynamics.

   - Accent the first note of a motive that ends softly.
   - Accent the last note of a motive that gets louder.
   - Play a legato motive that ends softly.
   - Play a legato line with a crescendo and a diminuendo.
   - Play a staccato motive that ends softly.
   - Play a staccato line with a crescendo.
   - Play a legato line with a crescendo.
   - Play a staccato line with a crescendo and a diminuendo.

4. Rhythm

- Play a phrase constructed primarily of quarter notes and eighth notes (metric).

- Play a phrase constructed primarily of long notes (supermetric).

- Play a phrase constructed primarily of short notes (submetric).

- Combine dynamics and articulation with metric, submetric, and supermetric phrases.

5. Melodic motion

- Conjunct. Play a shape constructed primarily of stepwise motion.

- Disjunct. Play a shape constructed primarily of skips.

6. Texture

- Single line. Play a single-line phrase.

- Harmonized line. Add harmony notes to the melody.

7. Harmony

- Diads. Play a phrase using two-note harmonizations.

- Clusters. Play a phrase using groups of notes that are close together.

Tip

When repeating a phrase in imitation, start the new phrase near in pitch to the resolution of the preceding phrase. This may help you maintain continuity in your thinking process.

Exercise 2. Adding Expression

Using the same blues progression, improvise a new solo, focusing on one element of expression throughout all motives in a chorus. For example, you might choose *diminuendo* as your expression. The process should be:

- Improvise a short, concise idea with a diminuendo at the end. Then rest.

- Imitate the shape, duration, rhythm, and articulation/dynamic of that idea. Then rest.

- Play a new shape. Then rest.

- Repeat the second shape that also has a diminuendo at the end. Then rest.

- Imitate the shape, duration, rhythm, and articulation/dynamic of the second shape. Then rest.

This is how your solo might turn out.

Exercise 3. Variations

As you play, organize your phrases in this structure:

- Play a short phrase that contains a crescendo-to-diminuendo. Then rest.
- Imitate the phrase. Then rest.
- Continue to the end of the chorus.

This is how your solo might turn out.

Critical Tools and Practice Method

Using this same process of playing, resting, and imitating, practice improvising using the following musical elements or techniques. For each one, play one entire chorus.

1. **Pitch Change.** Change the pitch level, but maintain the shape, rhythm, articulation, dynamic, and duration.

2. **Rhythmic Augmentation.** Expand the length of the motive by stretching out the rhythms. Either maintain or change the pitch level but augment the rhythms. Maintain the shape, articulation, and dynamic.

3. **Rhythmic Diminution.** Decrease the length of the phrase by contracting the rhythms, but maintain the shape and articulation/dynamic.

Phrase Placement

It is common to improvise using the same phrase placement as the original melody. In the example melody below, notice the pattern of phrases and rests.

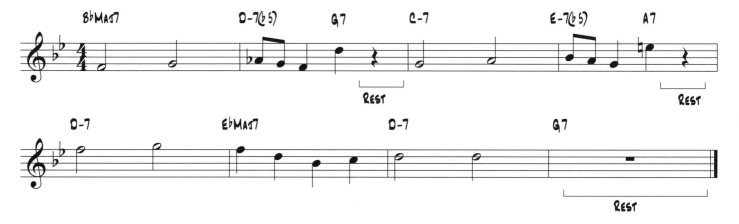

This improvisation matches the original melody's phrase placement.

Alternatively, you could deliberately offset some of the improvised phrases from the original melody. On the following page, the first phrase is delayed so that it overlaps with the second phrase of the melody.

Matching phrase structure is fine, but it can become too predictable if overdone. Practice beginning your improvisations both ways: matching and not matching the original melody. Here are some other ways to mix up the pacing:

- *Extended imitation/resolution.* Analyzed, this would be in the form *a* (idea), *a'*, *a''*, *a'''*, *b* (resolution). It can sound like an extended antecedent finally resolving to a consequent phrase.

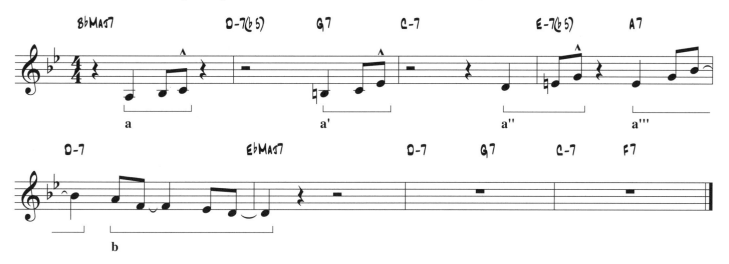

- *Extended fragment.* Analyzed, this would be in the form *a* (two-part idea), *b* (resolution, based on part of idea *a*), *b'*, *b''*, *b'''*. The varied fragment is often the end (resolution) of a two-part idea. This form can sound like multiple consequent phrases.

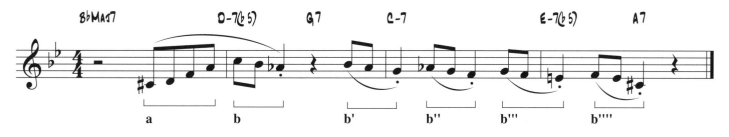

Tip: Phrase Placement

Keep your rhythmic phrasing from becoming predictable (for example, two measures of playing, two measures of rest) by sometimes adding longer rests. This will mix up the time, eliminate predictability, and help maintain musical interest. By hesitating before restating an idea, you can add a sense of expectation and excitement to the improvisation.

THEORY

Instinctive Improvisation

We have studied dozens of tools for creating and developing musical ideas. Some musical ideas, however, come from nowhere, arising from our subconscious minds. These can be the most powerful lines–the phrase shapes with the most musical merit, the lines most interesting to your musical ear, and the most fun to develop. They often seem to happen at turnarounds or other transitional points, where the intellectual mind is focused on moving to the next chord (or back to the top of the tune). The fingers just seem to "spit something out" instinctually.

These instinctive ideas are often generated from the chord changes and are often longer than the short motives we have been studying. The challenge is then to remember and imitate their shape. Putting such an interesting shape over the next set of chord changes adds tension and continuity to your playing. It also helps develop technique, as your fingers work to play something that was not conceived to go along with a set of chords.

Here's an example of an "instinctive line" occurring at a turnaround.

This angular and rhythmically articulate line covers the entire turnaround. Then, the solo returns to the top of the form, where there are two measures of CMaj7. Playing that same linear shape in this new context makes it sound rather wild and chromatic, for such a tame chord–certainly, something we'd not "think of" playing at this point in the tune.

Imitation combines aural and muscle memory. Our ears focus on the shape. Our fingers remember the feel of what they played, and they do it again. No analysis, no computer needed. It's simply an aural/physical response.

The idea improvised at the turnaround was created purely by subconscious instinct. The fingers just grooved over the changes. Then, the intellect said, "Repeat that, please." So, we play it again, but over a harmonic setting where we ordinarily might not think to play such a thing. Yet, it has a wonderful, driving effect at the top of the tune.

Guide your intuition with your intellect. This combination can yield powerful musical results.

PRACTICE

In these exercises, practice imitating those instinctual phrase shapes that you played at the turnarounds. On each of the following progressions, use the following approach.

1. The first time through, rest or comp until you reach the turnaround.

2. At the turnaround, play anything that comes to mind.

3. Back at the top, imitate that idea somewhere within the first four measures. Time permitting, imitate it again.

4. When you reach two measures prior to the turnaround, rest.

5. At the turnaround, blow another idea. Then imitate that new idea back at the top.

Continue this exercise until you feel in control of imitating those instinctual ideas played at the turnaround.

Exercise 1. Intuition Practice

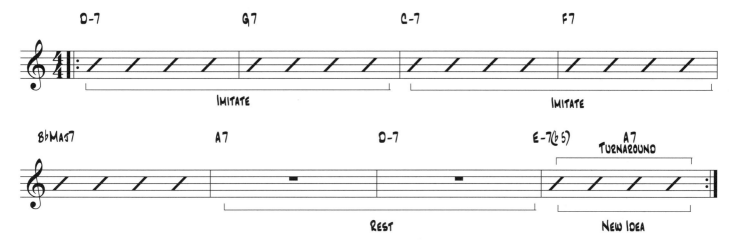

Exercise 2. Intuition Practice

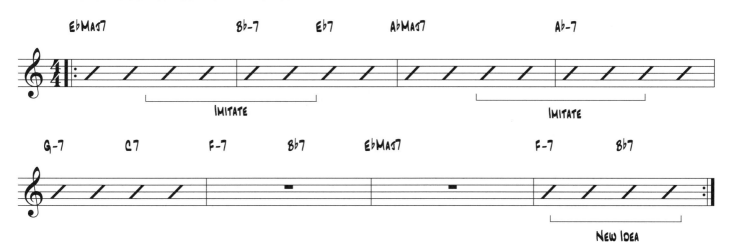

Exercise 3. Intuition Practice

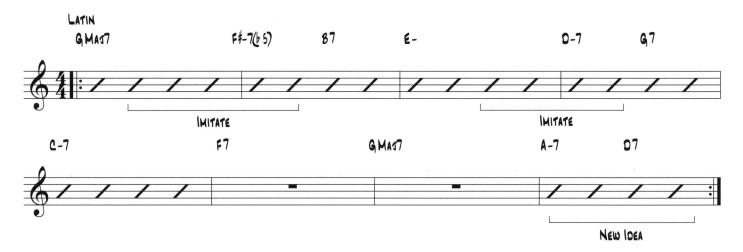

Exercise 4. Intuition Practice. Practice the next three practice progressions as before, but play longer phrases at the turnaround, and imitate them at the top.

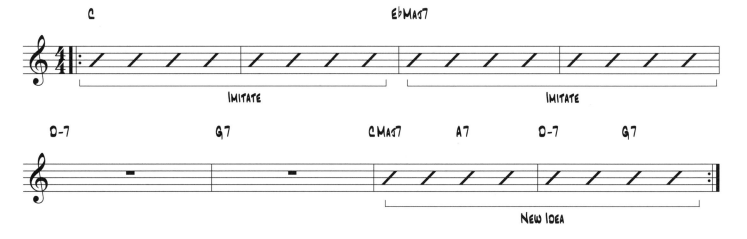

Exercise 5. Intuition Practice

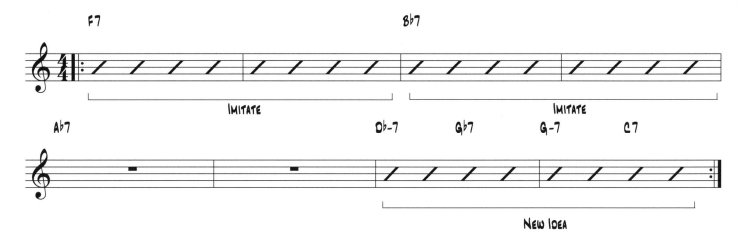

Exercise 6. Intuition Practice

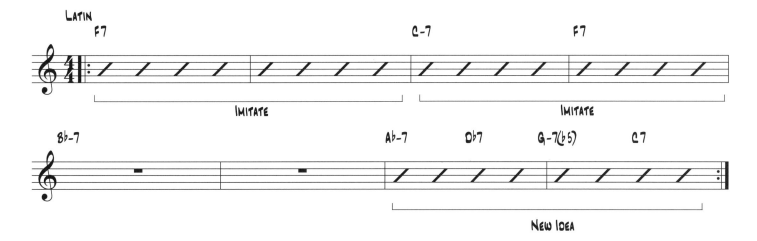

Mixing Long and Short Phrases

Use this process.

1. Play a short, concise phrase. Then rest.

2. Imitate the phrase. Then rest.

3. Play a long phrase. Then rest.

4. Imitate the shape and character of that longer idea. Then rest.

5. Continue, mixing up shorter and longer phrases. Strive towards imitating every single note that you play.

You may notice that your lines are quite different than those you're used to playing. Thinking primarily about the shape and character of lines often yields a different vocabulary than what you may be used to.

THEORY

Pitch Gradation

You can add a sense of organic development to a solo by paying close attention to the gradual ascent in overall pitch in the improvised melody. Most melodies end in the alto or soprano range. Beginning your improvised solo in the lower tenor region will distinguish its starting point. From there, slowly ascending up the keyboard will create a subliminal sense of overall form and direction. It may also add a subtle creative impetus to the improvised line.

The solo in "Suitable Love" uses pitch gradation as an organizing tool. "Dig Deep" is another good example of these techniques. (Both etudes are found later this lesson.) The asterisks mark the highest pitches of each phrase.

Method

The following approach will help you develop facility using pitch gradation in your solos.

1. Begin your solo in the tenor register. Play a short, concise phrase, and be careful to recognize and remember its highest note. Then rest.

2. Play another phrase, and include a note slightly higher than the high note of phrase 1. Then rest.

3. Repeat this process. Play short phrases followed by rests. Keep track of the highest note in each phrase, gradually increasing the pitch throughout your solo.

Continue this process for as long as it provides impetus to your solo. Remember, you may improvise freely below the highest pitch of each phrase.

For Deeper Practice

Move more slowly up the keyboard, separating the highest pitch of each phrase by only a second or a third. Using smaller intervals between the highest pitches will expand the time and the form of your solo.

TUNES

Etude. "Suitable Love"

"Suitable Love" is based on the chord changes to "Beautiful Love" by Victor Young. It illustrates the pitch gradation concept. Observe the motivic development and dynamic expression. Analyze the pitch gradation of the solo by circling the highest note of each phrase. Then practice it.

Suitable Love

Neil Olmstead

Etude. "Dig Deep"

"Dig Deep" is based on the chord changes to "Everything I Love" by Cole Porter. This piece begins with a right-hand part built by motivic development. The first phrase is a three-note motive that is repeated in the second measure at a different pitch level, with an added pickup note. In measure 6, there is an ascending scalewise motive that is truncated (shortened) in its development. In measure 7, the motive's shape is altered, while the rhythm is retained.

In this piece, a short fragment at the end of a phrase is developed. For example, the phrase shape in measure 12 is ascending/descending. The descending portion only is developed in measures 13 and 14. In the second chorus (m. 33), motivic development is less prevalent. However, the ends of many of the "complete phrases" are developed. The fragments that conclude these phrases are repeated (e.g., mm. 39–40, 42–43, 49, and 52–54).

The left-hand motives contain mixed rhythms of half and quarter notes, all within a quarter-time groove (such as the suspension in m. 6). In the second chorus (m. 33), the time settles into a fixed quarter-note accompaniment, as the right-hand solo breaks into a more free-flowing improvisation.

Dig Deep

Neil Olmstead

Lead Sheet. "Dig Deep"

28

Practice "Dig Deep" from the lead sheet, using a combination of left-hand rhythms (whole, half, and quarter notes), all in a quarter-time feel. Focus on the motives in the right-hand line. Imitate what you played using the techniques used in this chapter. If you need to, simplify your left hand, playing just whole and half notes, but keep the time. When your right hand is not imitating, try some shorter motives and phrases.

When listening to your favorite jazz artists, listen for motivic development by focusing on the contour, rhythms, articulation, and dynamics of each phrase. See how often the phrases are repeated. Then listen to a Mozart piano sonata. Listen for the same imitative characteristics. Do you hear similar characteristics being imitated in the jazz material and the classical material?

DIG DEEP

NEIL OLMSTEAD

Appendix A. Biographies

Lennie Tristano

Leonard Joseph Tristano was born in Chicago on March 19, 1919. His eyesight deteriorated slowly until the age of six, at which point he was totally blind. Nevertheless, he studied music extensively, including at the American Conservatory of Music.

From the age of twelve, he played piano in various settings and led his own Dixieland group as a clarinetist. Later, he played tenor saxophone and clarinet, as well as piano, in a rumba band. A year after making his first recordings in 1945, Tristano moved to New York. In the years that followed, he worked successfully to expand the harmonic horizons of jazz improvisation. His early influences included Earl Hines and Art Tatum, but eventually, he became the leader of an informal cult—a school of progressive musical ideas. Critics characterized Lennie Tristano as one of the most interesting musicians in the field of "cool jazz."

In June, 1951, Lennie opened his own studio, the Tristano School of Music. Teaching was a primary activity for him, and several well-known musicians came to him for instruction, including John LaPorta, Sal Mosca, Lee Konitz, Warne Marsh, Bud Freeman, and Bob Wilbur.

Leonard Feather called Tristano "one of the most determinedly radical thinkers in modern jazz." *(The Encyclopedia of Jazz.* New York: Horizon Press, 1960.) Alfons Dauer, the German jazz critic, called Lennie's type of music "the most abstract and intellectual in modern jazz, as well as being absolutely uncompromising and noncommercial." (Ulanov, Barry. *The New Tristano* [Liner Notes]. Atlantic LP, 1962.)

When Tristano eventually stopped performing in the late 1960s, his impact on the scene declined somewhat. Yet, since his death in 1978, we find that his singular style and influence is one that has yet to be matched.

Dave McKenna

Dave McKenna was born in Woonsocket, Rhode Island in 1930. His early playing experiences included stints with the Woody Herman Orchestra and Boots Mussuli. This led to performances in the fifties and sixties with Zoot Sims, Al Cohn, Stan Getz and Bobby Hacket, and later with Scott Hamilton and Jake Hanna. He became well known as a solo pianist while gigging at the Columns on Cape Cod and the Copley Plaza Bar in Boston. The author had the good fortune to open for McKenna during this long engagement at the Copley Plaza Bar in the eighties.

In addition to numerous quartet CDs, McKenna has a large solo and duo piano discography that illustrates his wonderful earthy, driving swing that is set up with a deep rhythmic bass line. McKenna is a lover of tunes, and the melodies in his arrangements often show this. His solo performances reveal how he often alters the time, moving from a ballad feel to swing and then back to cut time—freely, yet in a way that clearly embellishes the song as a whole. The beautiful melodies of the *American Song Book* are stated and then developed in improvisations that are always melodically logical, joyful, and unencumbered with intellect. All this is interspersed with chords that seem to appear and then disappear somewhere in the middle, yet never inhibiting the overriding contrapuntal texture of his improvisations.

Dave McKenna passed away in 2008.

Appendix B. Discography

Listen to the following selections from LPs and CDs. Transcribe and analyze the solos, in full or partially. Try to absorb the rhythmic and melodic concepts of "the masters."

Baron, Kenny and Stan Getz. *People Time.* Verve double CD 510823-2, 1991.
    "Like Someone in Love"
    "Softly as in a Morning Sunrise"
    "Surrey with the Fringe on Top"

Broadbent, Alan. *Alan Broadbent/Gary Foster.* Concord Records CCD-4562, 1993.
    Duo performance recorded live at Maybeck Recital Hall.
    "Ode to the Road"
    "317 East 32nd Street"
    "What is This Thing Called Love/Subconcious-Lee"
    "If You Could See Me Now" (Contrapuntal solo)
    "In Your Own Sweet Way"

Crothers, Connie. *Solo.* Jazz Records JR4LP, 1980. Live solo concert.
    "That Straight Ahead Thing"
    "Love Suite: Roy Eldridge, Sheila Jordan, Max Roach"

Davis, Miles. Red Garland, piano. *'Round About Midnight.* Columbia CK40610, 1955.
—*Steamin' with the Miles Davis Quintet.* Prestige 7200, 1956.
—*Workin' with the Miles Davis Quintet.* Prestige 7166, 1956.
—*Relaxin' with the Miles Davis Quintet.* Prestige 7129, 1956.

Evans, Bill. *Best of Bill Evans.* Verve LP V6-8747, 1963. Three pianos, originally released on Verve, *Conversations With Myself.*
    "How About You"
—*Undercurrent.* Blue Note, CDP 7905832, 1962. Duo album with Jim Hall, guitar.
    "My Funny Valentine" (Bass and chords)
—*Mary McPartland's Piano Jazz.* The Jazz Alliance TJA-12004, 1978. Interview and performance with Bill Evans.
    "In Your Own Sweet Way"
—*How My Heart Sings.* Riverside 25218, 1962.
    "In Your Own Sweet Way" (Take 1, 2). Exemplifies use of guide tones as inner voice arrangement of head.

Garland, Red. See "Davis, Miles."

Hawes, Hampton. *The Challenge.* Storyville (1968).

Krall, Diana. *When I Look in Your Eyes.* Verve, IMPD-304, 1991.
    "I Can't Give You Anything But Love"

McKenna, Dave. *Dancing in the Dark (and other music of Arthur Schwartz).* Concord Jazz, Inc. 1986.
    "You and the Night and the Music"
    "Dancing in the Dark"
    "A Gal in Calico"

—*Giant Strides,* Concord Jazz, Inc. LP CJ99, 1979.
    "Lulu's Back in Town"
    "Love Letters"
    "Yardbird Suite"
    "Walkin' My Baby Back Home"
—*By Myself.* Shiah Records, LP, 1976.
    "No More Ouzo for Puzo"
    "'A' Train"
—*Double Play; No Bass Hit/Major League.* Concord Jazz, 2002.
—*The Piano Scene of Dave McKenna.* Epic, 1958. (Later released as *This Is the Moment.)*
—*Left Handed Complement.* Concord Jazz, 1979.
—*Piano Mover.* Concord Jazz, 1979.

Mehldau, Brad. *The Art of the Trio, Volume One.* Warner Brothers 46260, 1997.
    "Blackbird," "Nobody Else But Me" Trio
—*Songs (The Art of the Trio, Volume Three).* Warner Brothers 47051, 1998.
    "Unrequited" Trio
    "At a Loss" Trio
—*Introducing.* Warner Brothers 45997, 1995.
    "Young Werther" Trio

Monteliu, Tete. *Boston Concert.* Steeple Chase Records and Tapes SCM51125/3, 1981.
    "Giant Steps" (Up)
    "Hot House"

Peterson, Oscar. *In a Mellow Mood.* BASF LP H25156, 1973. Live trio LP with Bob Durham and Sam Jones.
    "Sandy's Blues" (Intro to trio)

Petrucciani, Michel. *Solo Piano.* Blue Note CDP 0777, 1993.
    "C Jam Blues"

Tristano, Lennie. *The New Tristano.* Atlantic LP 1357, 1962.
    "Becoming"
    "C-Minor Complex" (Free form)
    "You Don't Know What Love Is" by Ray/DePaul
    "Deliberation" (based on "Indiana" by J. Hanley)
    "Scene and Variations"
        a. Carol
        b. Tania
        c. Bud
    "Love Lines"
    "G-Minor Complex" (Free form)
—*Lennie Tristano featuring Lee Konitz.* Giants of Jazz CD53155, 2001. This is a reissue of LP *The New Tristano.* It also includes:
    "You Don't Know What Love Is"
    "Rehearsal from Recording Date" (based on "It's You or No One" by J. Styne)
—*Lennie Tristano.* Jazz Record Series, Rhino Records R271595, 1994. Has all *The New Tristano* material except "C Minor Complex." Also contains trio and quartet material from 1956.

—*Concert in Copenhagen.* Jazz Records JR12CD, 1997. Live solo piano concert.
   "Lullaby of the Leaves"
   "Tivoli Gardens"
   "It's You or No One" (Head only vaguely implied)

Zeitlan, Denny, *Cathexis.* Columbia, CS8982, 1964. Trio
   "Blue Phoenix" (Free form)
—*Carnival.* Columbia, CS 9140, 1965. Trio

Appendix C. Modes and Jazz Scales

The following is a list of common modes and jazz scales and their corresponding chords.

Chord	Mode/Scale
Major 7	Ionian, Lydian
Minor 7	Dorian, Aeolian, Phrygian
Dominant 7	Mixolydian, Lydian ♭7, Altered
Minor 7(♭5)	Locrian, Aeolian ♭5

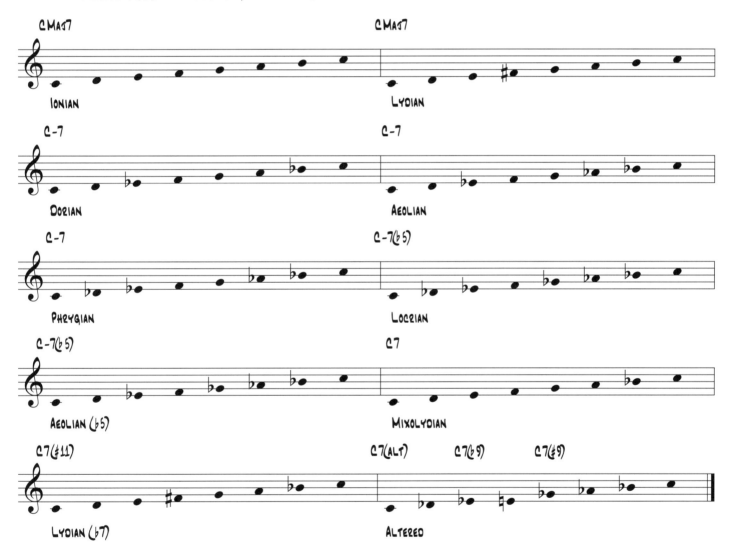

The following chords and scales are less common. These scales are sometimes referred to as *synthetic scales*.

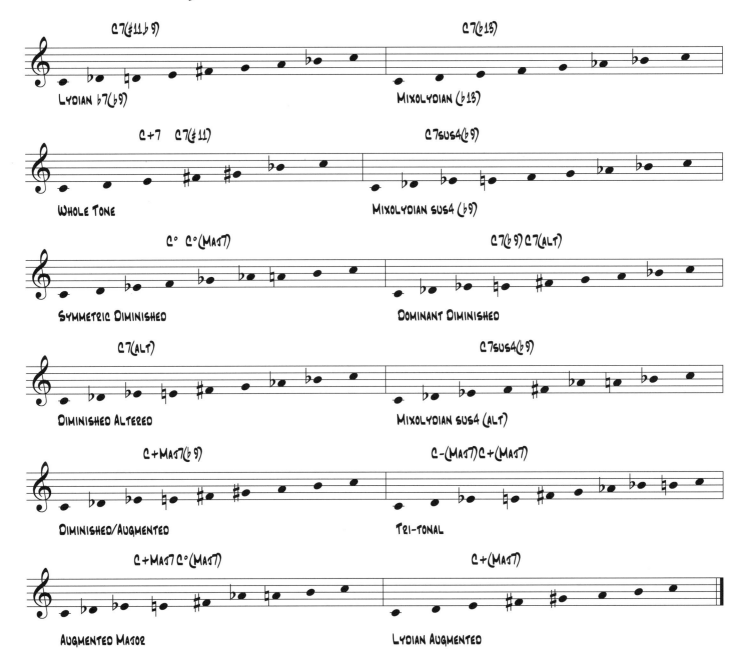

Appendix D. Linear Independence Exercises

These exercises are designed to improve your sense of swing and your flexibility in improvising against a bass line. The major key exercises are based on the Mixolydian mode superimposed upon two-five progressions. The minor exercises are based on the harmonic minor mode.

The Mixolydian exercises contain chromatic notes that allow the chord tones of the dominant seventh chord to fall on the beat. All the lines can be displaced by one, two, or sometimes three beats, still allowing the scale to be "functional" on all chords.

How to Practice

Play all these exercises in all keys, descending chromatically.

Use a metronome on beats 2 and 4 to help your sense of time and groove. The half note may equal 40 to 120. Start slowly so that you can focus on the depth of your swing. Try to hold back or "stretch" the rhythm of the eighths.

Displace all lines by one or two beats, as illustrated.

Play just half-note root-five motives in your left hand. Eventually, you will be able to improvise your own bass lines, becoming as involved as you wish. But now, the primary goal is to practice your sense of rhythm while playing against a bass line. Repeat each line as necessary in order to relax with the groove. Then, you can modulate.

MAJOR KEY EXERCISES

Exercise 1. Major

This exercise is based on the Mixolydian mode with an antecedent-consequent ending. Continue it through all keys.

Exercise 2. Major

This exercise is a syncopated version of exercise 1. Note that in exercises 1 and 2, the chord tones of the dominant chord are placed on the beat.

Exercise 3. Major

This exercise starts on the second degree of the Mixolydian mode, but contains a chromatic, which allows all chord tones (of C7) to fall on the beat.

Exercise 4. Major

This syncopated line moves from the second degree but has a chromatic seventh of the C Mixolydian mode.

Exercise 5. Major

This line moves from the third degree of the Mixolydian mode, contains a chromatic (♭9), and has a substitute note (4th) for what would be a chromatic (7th).

Exercise 6. Major

This line begins on the fourth degree of the Mixolydian mode and has a substitute note for the ♭9 chromatic (in this case 5), yet retains the next chromatic (7).

Tip

As you become comfortable with the right-hand lines, try improvising your own left-hand figures staying within the *root-five* and *root-chromatic* context.

Exercise 7. Major

This exercise contains a triplet that is substituting for a chromatic, which would ordinarily be placed on the flat-third degree. The walking line in the left hand is constructed of roots, fifths, and chromatic approaches. As you continue through all keys, you may find it easier to improvise your own left-hand line using these elements.

MINOR KEY EXERCISES

These exercises are based on the tonic harmonic minor scale. This scale may be superimposed upon the dominant chord.

As before, play these exercises in all keys, and use a metronome. Focus on the right-hand line—its transposition and groove. Keep your left hand simple, in order not to lose the time, and focus on making it swing. Use half-note motives, or play simpler root-five motives in quarter notes.

Exercise 1. Minor

This exercise illustrates the ascending left-hand motive built on the Locrian mode (ii-7[♭5]). The root-five motive of measure 3 breaks up the motion before going on to the descending motive in the Lydian mode (VIMaj7). The right-hand line is centered on the tonic's harmonic minor scale. However, the chord tones of the dominant chord fall on the beat, as they did in the major-key exercises.

Exercise 2. Minor

Exercises 2 and 3 have only half notes in the left hand and may be played at a faster tempo.

Exercise 3. Minor

Try displacing this line to start on beats 3 and 4.

Exercise 4. Minor

In this exercise, a secondary dominant arpeggio precedes a descending harmonic minor scale that is displaced by one beat upon its repeat. The comping figures between the lines are optional. Feel free to create your own voicings. Try displacing to beat 3 as well.

Scales That Move from Major to Minor

The Mixolydian scale of a major key (e.g., C Mixolydian for the key of F) can be used in the relative minor with only the last note changing (C Mixolydian ending on a C-sharp).

In all keys, practice these lines, which move from major to minor. Improvise a bass line in your left hand. Change your metronome marking frequently, moving from medium to slow to fast. Focus on the swing. Try displacing to beats 3 and 4 as well.

MAJOR TO MINOR EXERCISES

Exercise 1. Major to Minor

Exercise 2. Major to Minor

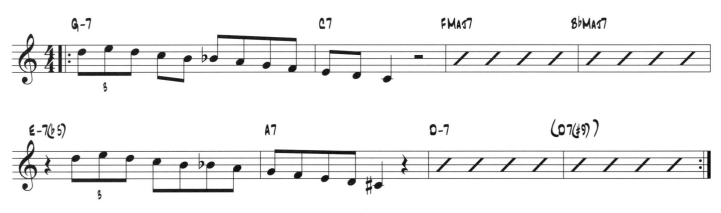

Exercise 3. Major to Minor

Exercise 4. Major to Minor

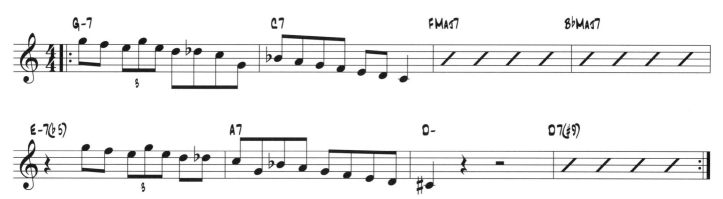

Exercise 5. Major to Minor

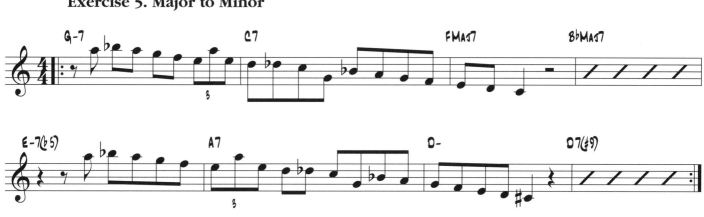

Appendix E. Master Tune List

The tunes in this book are based on chord progressions from the jazz standards repertoire. Learning the original tune, in addition to studying the etude or lead sheet, will help you improve your understanding of the topics in each chapter.

STANDARDS	ETUDES/LEAD SHEETS
Chapter 1. Fundamentals of Chord Theory	
"I Fall in Love Too Easily" by Jerome Kern	"So Easily"
Chapter 2. Chord Extensions	
"I Fall in Love Too Easily" by Jerome Kern	"So Easily: Take 2"
"I Wish I Knew" by Harry Warren	"I Had a Clue"
"Green Dolphin Street" by Kaper/Washington	"Sweet Dolphin Suite"
Chapter 3. Half-Note Motives	
"Night and Day" by Cole Porter	"A Night at Play"
Chapter 4. Ballad To Swing	
"Laura" by Mercer/Raksin	"Flora"
"The Days of Wine and Roses" by Henry Mancini	"Cabernet"
Chapter 5. Walking Bass	
"I Remember You" by Mercer/Schertzinger	"I Remember Soo"
"How Deep Is the Ocean" by Irving Berlin	"How Deep Is Emotion"
Chapter 6. Linear Motives	
"My Shining Hour" by Mercer/Arlen	"Flying Towers"
"You and the Night and the Music" by Dietz/Schwartz	"You Are in Flight with the Music"
"Love Letters" by Victor Young	"Dove Feathers"
"If I Should Lose You" by Ralph Rainger	"Winds of Kyle"
Chapter 7. The Jazz Waltz	
"Up with the Lark" by Irving Berlin	"Spring Cardinal"
"Summer Night" by Harry Warren	"Summer Flight"
Chapter 8. Compound Lines	
"Golden Earrings" by Victor Young	"Golden Feelings"
"Like Someone in Love" by Jimmy Van Heusen	"Wild Bill"
Chapter 9. Embellishing the Bass Line	
"Nice Work If You Can Get It" by George Gershwin	"Go For It!"
"Funk in Deep Freeze" by Hank Mobley	"Zee Deep Freeze"
"In Her Own Sweet Way" by Dave Brubeck	"In Her Sleek Way"

Chapter 10. Pedal Point
"It Could Happen to You" by Jimmy Van Heusen "Consequences"
"All of You" by Cole Porter "Evan's Up"
"I'll Take Romance" by Oscar Hammerstein "Take a Breath"

Chapter 11. The Blues and Beyond
"I Got Rhythm" by George Gershwin "Bop Stop"

Chapter 12. Triads
"Nobody Else But Me" by Jerome Kern "Dave's Delight"

Chapter 13. The Latin Connection
"O Grande Amour" by Antonio Carlos Jobim "The Big Love"

Chapter 14. Guide-Tone Lines
"Old Folks" by Willard Robison "Old Coats"

Chapter 15. Non-Chord Tones
"Softly, As in a Morning Sunrise" by Sigmund Romberg "Laura Lightly"

Chapter 16. Melody in the Middle
"Whisper Not" by " by Benny Golson "DAO"

Chapter 17. Rhythmic Freedom
"Alone Together" by Dietz/Schwartz "Singularity"

Chapter 18. Melodic Freedom
"Yesterdays" by Jerome Kern "Jester Play"

Chapter 19. Tristano Techniques
"Solar" by Miles Davis "Ultra Violet"

Chapter 20. Metric Modulation
"All the Things You Are" by Jerome Kern "All the Tongs"
"Some Day My Prince Will Come" by Frank Churchill "Green Tea"

Chapter 21. Motivic Development and Imitation
"Beautiful Love" by Victor Young "Suitable Love"
"Everything I Love" by Cole Porter "Everything I Dig"

Glossary

abbreviated pedal: a sustained root or fifth in the bass occurring with other activity in the left hand; a short pedal point

altered tension: extension of a chord that is chromatically raised or lowered (e.g., ♭9, ♯9, ♭13)

alternate fingers: using a different finger on a repeated note (e.g., 1-3-1)

alternate motive: stepwise ascending diatonic motive on a two-five progression

antecedent/consequent: two-phrase structure with a question/answer quality

anticipated triplet: a motive where the root of the upcoming chord begins a triplet embellishing motive

appoggiatura: a non-chord tone that is leapt into and resolved by step in the opposite direction

arrow sheet: a lead sheet with arrows indicating the direction the bass line will go

articulation: characteristics of a note including accents, dynamics, and duration

augmentation: expansion of an interval or rhythm

aural memory: remembering what we hear

binary meter: a time signature that is divisible by two (e.g., 2/4, 4/4)

blues motive: a leap up or down to the third of a chord from the root

bop period: roughly the 1940s (also *bebop* period)

bossa nova: a common Latin rhythm

changes: chords, usually indicated by symbols

chord tones: tones making up a chord

chorus: one complete time through a tune, usually 32 measures

chromatic approach: half step motion to a chord tone; *upper* chromatic approaches are above the chord tone, *lower* chromatic approaches are below the chord tone

chromatically enhanced: a figure, such as pedal point, that is embellished by half steps on either side

cliché: a commonly heard line within a chord progression

cluster: a block of notes, usually within whole and half steps of each other, that sound simultaneously

comp: to play or playing chords as accompaniment (also *comping*)

complete phrases: improvised lines that are not in need of (or resist) development

compound line: a line that implies or contains a secondary line

concerted rhythm: simultaneously sounding rhythms between hands

conjunct: stepwise

consecutive triplet motive: an embellishing motive containing two triplets

contour: the shape and direction of a line

cut time: a two-beat meter; half-time

cycle-five motion: chord root motion a fifth apart

descending passing tone: a non-chord tone approached and left by step in downward motion

diad: a two-note chord

diminution: intervalic or rhythmic contraction of a line

disjunct: non-stepwise motion; leaps

dominant pedal: a pedal point on the fifth degree of a key

double time: exactly twice the tempo written

double-time feel: implying twice the tempo within a constant meter

elision: the connection of two phrases by one note at which the resolution of one phrase is the start of the next

etude: through-composed study

fifth motive: using the fifth of the chord as an embellishing note

free counterpoint: left-hand improvisation that moves away from the prescribed motives

functional motive: a prescribed motive that outlines the harmony

groove: the rhythmic emotive quality of a tune

harmonic rhythm: the general rhythm of a chord progression

harmonized line: a right-hand line that contains harmony

head: the melody

horizontal playing: using motives and lines for improvisational inspiration

imitation/variation: repetition of a musical idea, with possible modifications

incipient phrase: a short incomplete idea

jazz waltz: a jazz tune in 3/4 time

key area: a tonal region of a tune

kick: an embellishing left-hand eighth note

Latin groove: a straight eighth-note rhythm

lead sheet: a score containing chords and melody only

linking pedal: connecting pedal points

mambo: a common Latin rhythm

metric modulation: changing meter within a tune

modal playing: improvising primarily on the modes

motive: a short concise phrase that requires development

multivoice improvisation: improvising more than one line simultaneously, usually with bass accompaniment

muscle memory: subconscious memory of the fingers

neighbor tone: a non-chord tone that is approached and left by step in opposite directions

non-chord tone: any note that is not in the fundamental chord

octave kick: an embellishing motive that uses the root at the lower octave

octave-third: an embellishing motive that uses the third in two octaves

out playing: free improvisation usually devoid of form and harmony

passing tone: a non-chord tone that is approached and left by step in the same direction

pedal point: a sustained tone in the bass, usually the tonic or dominant of a tonal area

pickup note: a note leading into a strong beat (anacrusis)

pitch gradation: an improvisation study method wherein the solo line gradually ascends in pitch

quarter time: 4/4 time

repeated note motive: used as an embellishing motive

returning note motive: returning to the root as an embellishing motive

rhythm changes: a chord progression based on Gershwin's "I Got Rhythm"

rhythmic displacement: repeating a motive or line at a different starting point within a measure

rhythmic modulation: changing the groove within a metric modulation

right-hand coordinated triplet: an embellishing motive using both hands

rubato: slow, free playing within the phrase form of the piece

samba: a common Latin rhythm

scale of the moment: a scale assigned to a brief tonal area within a tune

sequence: a repeated and connected motive or phrase shape

shape: relating to the contour and rhythm of a line

straight eighth notes: non-swing eighth notes

swing eighth notes: eighth notes played as in a triplet rhythm (e.g., the scat syllables "oo-ba")

suspension: any chord tone or tension that is tied into the next chord and resolves down or up by step

temporal development: development of the music's time

temporal form: using time to assist in an arrangement

tension substitution: a chord tension used as substitute for a chord tone

tension: extension of a chord (e.g., 9, 11, 13)

tertial rhythm: 3/4 meter

tessitura: a range of notes used to improvise

through composed: completely written out

tonal area: key region of a tune

tonal modulation: moving from one key to another

tonic pedal: using the tonic note of the key in a pedal point

triplet motives: embellishing motives containing triplets

truncated: a shortened line, motive, or form

turnaround: a progression used at the end of a tune or section that leads back to the beginning of the tune or section (e.g., I VI II V)

two-five: the second chord of the scale (II–7) followed by the fifth chord of the scale (V7)

vertical playing: improvising while thinking primarily of the chords

vocabulary: tonal language used in improvisation

voice leading: chord tones that are moving smoothly from one chord to the next

voicings: the arrangement of the notes within a chord structure

About the Author

Neil Olmstead is an active jazz pianist, teacher, and composer. A recently released jazz duo album is titled *Colaboração*. Neil's symphonic compostitions have been recorded by the Warsaw National Philharmonic Orchestra and the Bratislava Radio Television Orchestra. During a ten-year solo piano residency at Boston's Copley Plaza Hotel, Neil opened for Teddy Wilson, Dave McKenna, and Adam Makowicz, among others.

Neil holds a bachelor of music from Berklee College of Music and a master of music from New England Conservatory, and studied composition with Nadia Boulanger in Fontainebleau, France. Neil is currently professor of piano at Berklee College of Music in Boston.